英語学習者のための英文法

PRACTICE MAKES PERFECT
English Grammar for ESL Learners

Ed Swick 著

伊藤淳一 訳

文芸社

contents

はしがき

多くの人々は文法を学ぶことを雑用だと思っております。時には、そうであるかもしれません。それはさておき、どんな言語の文法でも理解するには、その言語の熟練者となり正確な使用者になることが絶対に必要です。英語ももちろん例外ではありません。

語学学習者のための文法規則は、ドライバーのための交通規則のようなものです。きちんと運転し、他のドライバーと共に走行できるようになるためには、すべての人が従う規則を知らなければなりません。もちろん、規則を破って、他のドライバーに迷惑をかける運転をする人もいます。それはまた言語にも当てはまります。文法の規則に従っていれば、自分の言いたいことをはっきりと表現できます。しかし、それらの規則を守り損なうと、人々はその人を理解するのが難しいと思うかもしれませんし、あるいは、完全に誤解さえしてしまうかもしれません。そういう観点からしても、文法を正しく理解し使用することは、本当に、非常に重要なことなのです。

ところで、文法とは一体何なのでしょうか？　ファンクとワグナルズのNew College Standard Dictionary（ニューカレッジ標準辞書）には、文法について"特定の言語の口述あるいは書面による使用のさまざまな原理を説明する科学の一種"のように説明した上で、さらにまた"特定の言語を正確に話したり書いたりする発達した芸術"とも述べております。科学であろうと芸術であろうと、文法は、言語の正しい使い方を説明する記述から成り立っています。例えば、

Description: Begin a sentence with *do* to change a statement to a question.

説明文：平叙文を疑問文に変えるにはdoを使って文を始めてください。

Usage: Statement = "You understand the problem."

使用方法：平叙文 = "あなたはこの問題を理解しています。"

Question = "*Do* you understand the problem?"

疑問文 = "あなたはこの問題を理解していますか。"

あるいは：

Description: Use *he* as the subject of a sentence; use *him* as the direct object.

説明文：文の主語としてheを用いなさい；直接目的語としてhimを用いなさい。

Usage: Subject = "*He* is a good friend of mine."

使用方法：主語 = "彼は私の仲のいい友だちです。"

Direct Object = "I visit *him* very often."

直接目的語 = "私は彼を非常にしばしば訪ねます。"

このような文法的な説明文は多くあり、それぞれが英語を正しく形成し使用する方法の知識の構造での基本要素となっています。習得している基本要素の数が多ければ多いほど、話し言葉

や書き言葉の正確さが向上するでしょう。

標準文法は英語の伝統的な規則で構成されています。標準文法こそが、文法学者や英語教授が、誰もが話したり書いたりする時に使ってもらいたいと望んでいるものなのです。しかし、言語というものは時が経つにつれ進化し、そして英語圏で続いていることと伝統的な規則とは、時には、歩調を乱すようなのです。より最新の、または人気のある使用法が、タメ語と呼ばれることがあります。タメ語とは、人々が日常生活で現実に話している言葉で、しばしば標準文法と直接的に矛盾します。実例として、標準文法では、文の主語としてはwhoを使用すべきであり、文の目的語として使用する場合はwhomを使うべきであるとしています。しかし、タメ語では必ずしもそうなってはおりません。例えば、

Standard grammar: "Whom did you visit in New York?"
Casual language: "Who did you visit in New York?"

意味は、標準文法（上の文）でも、タメ語（下の文）でも「あなたはニューヨークで誰を訪ねましたか」の意味になります。

上の例文が、文法的により優れていると思われますが、下の例文が、より一般的に使われております。

別の種類の例では、動詞diveが関与しております。この動詞の過去時制は、規則的（dived）か不規則的（dove）かのどちらかです。違いは何ですか？　基本的に、何もありません。どちらの形も過去時制として正しく使われています。だが、英語は日々進化しています。状況も変化しております。そして英語圏が、動詞*dive*の過去時制が、規則的であるべきか不規則的であるべきか、どちらを望んでいるかを決めるのです。その決定がどうなるかを知るのにかなり長い時間がかかるかもしれません。とりあえず、しばらくは、過去時制でdivedとdoveの両方を聞き続けることになります。

動詞proveにもよく似たケースがあります。今日、多くの人が完了時制の分詞としてprovedを用います："He has proved「彼は証明してしまった」あるいは "We had not proved「私たちは証明していませんでした」"しかし、今日、provedの代わりに、形容詞として一般に認められている古風な形（proven）を今でも用いている別の人々もおります："He has proven「彼は証明されています」あるいは "We had not proven.「私たちは証明されていませんでした」"のように。

ここのポイントは、文法規則が、より良い英語を話したり書いたりする方向に導いてくれていることです。しかし、文法の多くの規則は、特定のカジュアルな、人気のある用法によって破壊され、言語が変遷状態にあるため他のものも依然として不明確になっていることです。これ

らの離脱がどこで起こっているのか、それらがこの本で論じられるでしょう。というのは、もし英語学習者が、who を文の主語として用いるだけの用法しか知らなかったとしたら、その人たちは次のようなタメ語の文が出てきたら困惑させられてしまうでしょう：例えば、"Who did you visit in New York?「あなたはニューヨークで誰を訪ねたのですか」"のような。

しかしながら、ただ文法規則を知るだけでは不十分なのです。この本はまた、英文法を使用する際に、豊富な練習問題を提供しています。練習すればするほど、ますます英語の使用法や理解度が熟達します。さまざまな角度から英語を巧みに操れるようになるためのさまざまな練習問題があります。この本の最後にあるアンサーキーは、正しい解答ばかりではなく、練習問題をどうやって完成させるかについても提案します。

英文法は、必ずしも雑用ではありません。それどころか、英文法は、非常に豊富な財宝の扉を開けるカギとなり得ます。

〈※は、訳者注記です。分かり難いところを簡単に説明を付記しました〉

Unit 1 | 名詞

名詞は固有にも普通にもなることができ、固有名詞は特定の人、場所、物、あるいはアイディアに言及します。そのような名詞は大文字で書き始めます：例えば、America, George Washington, Mr. Neruda, October.

特定の人、場所、物、あるいはアイディアに言及しない名詞を普通名詞と呼び、大文字で書き始めることもありません：例えば、land, girls, money, test. 固有名詞と普通名詞の下記のリストを比較してみてください。

固有名詞	普通名詞
Mexico（メキシコ）	country（国）
Ms. Finch（フィンチさん）	woman（女性）
English（英語）	language（言語）
McGraw-Hill（マグロウ・ヒル）	publisher（出版社）
American Airlines（アメリカン・エアラインズ）	company（会社）
December（12月）	month（月）

練習問題1-1

それぞれの名詞の隣にその語が固有名詞か、普通名詞かあてはまるものを書きなさい。

1、_____ France
2、_____ rope
3、_____ United States
4、_____ Professor
5、_____ professor
6、_____ the stadium
7、_____ the Olympics
8、_____ horses
9、_____ Dr. Blanchard
10、_____ our school

練習問題1-2

固有名詞は大文字にして、それぞれの名詞を書き直しなさい。

1、_____ glass
2、_____ rocky mountains
3、_____ mexico

4、＿＿＿＿＿＿＿＿＿＿＿＿＿＿＿＿＿＿＿＿＿＿＿＿＿　flowers

5、＿＿＿＿＿＿＿＿＿＿＿＿＿＿＿＿＿＿＿＿＿＿＿＿＿　bus

6、＿＿＿＿＿＿＿＿＿＿＿＿＿＿＿＿＿＿＿＿＿＿＿＿＿　the store

7、＿＿＿＿＿＿＿＿＿＿＿＿＿＿＿＿＿＿＿＿＿＿＿＿＿　new york times

8、＿＿＿＿＿＿＿＿＿＿＿＿＿＿＿＿＿＿＿＿＿＿＿＿＿　roberto

9、＿＿＿＿＿＿＿＿＿＿＿＿＿＿＿＿＿＿＿＿＿＿＿＿＿　professor romano

10、＿＿＿＿＿＿＿＿＿＿＿＿＿＿＿＿＿＿＿＿＿＿＿＿＿　my books

名詞は文の主語として用いることができます。主語は文中で動作を行わせている語です。主語は固有名詞あるいは普通名詞がなることができるし、単数形でも複数形にもなれます。

> *Juanita* is a friend of mine.　「ファニータは私の友だちの1人です」
> *The boys* like to play soccer.　「その少年たちはサッカーをするのが好きです」
> Where is the *school?*　　　　「学校はどこですか」

名詞はまた直接目的語として用いることができます。文中の直接目的語は動詞の動作を受ける名詞です。文中の直接目的語を見つけるために3つのことを行ってください。

　　1、文の主語を見つけなさい

　　2、文の動詞を見つけなさい

　　3、主語と動詞で誰を、または何かをたずねなさい

下の例文を見てください。

"Sara likes my brother."

1、主語＝ Sara（セイラ）

2、動詞＝ likes（好きである）

3、誰をたずねるのか＝

Whom does Sara like?

「セイラが好きなのは誰ですか」

「直接目的語は my brother（私の弟）」

"The girls find a book."

1、主語＝ girls（少女たち）

2、動詞＝ find（見つける）

3、何をたずねるのか＝

What do the girls find?

「少女たちは何を見つけようとしているのか」

「直接目的語は book（本）です」

名詞は時には間接目的語になります。間接目的語は文中で直接目的語の前に置かれます。「誰に、または誰のために」の対象になる人で、何かを直接目的語から提供される人です（※　S＋V＋IO［間接目的語］＋DO［直接目的語］の文型を考えてください）。文で間接目的語を見つけるためには3つのことを行ってください。

　　　　1、文の主語を見つけなさい

２、文の動詞を見つけなさい

　　３、主語と動詞で誰に、または誰のためにかをたずねなさい

それらの例文を見てください：

"Justin buys the girl a magazine."　　　　　　　"Mother gives Nate five dollars."
「ジャスティンは少女に雑誌を買う」　　　　　　「母はネイトに５ドル与える」
１、主語 = Justin　　　　　　　　　　　　　　　１、主語 = Mother
２、動詞 = buys　　　　　　　　　　　　　　　　２、動詞 = gives
３、誰に対して、誰のためにかをたずねなさい＝　　３、誰に対して、誰のためにかをたずねなさい
ジャスティンは誰のために雑誌を買うのか　　　　＝　母は誰に対して５ドル与えるのか

間接目的語はthe girl（少女）　　　　　　　　　　間接目的語は（Nate）ネイト

注釈：無生物が間接目的語として使われるのは珍しいことです。

名詞が叙述名詞として使われる時、その名詞は文中で述語の後に続きます。述部は動詞単独か、あるいは動詞句がなることができます：

　　述語としての動詞：Maria *helps* us.「マリアは我々を助ける」
　　述部としての動詞句：Maria *usually helps with the gardening*.「マリアはガーデニングをす
　　　　　　　　　るのをいつも手伝ってくれる」
述語名詞は、非常に頻繁にbeやbecome動詞の後に続きます。

　　My mother wants to be *a doctor*.　　　「母は医者になりたいと思っている」
　　Celine became *an actress*.　　　　　　「セリーヌは女優になった」
　　Are you *the manager* of this building?　「この建物の支配人はあなたですか」

練習問題1-3
それぞれの文のイタリック体で書かれた語を見て、その語がどのように使われているかを決めて、それから空欄に、主語、直接目的語、間接目的語、叙述名詞のいずれかを書きなさい。

1、＿＿＿＿＿＿＿＿＿＿＿＿＿＿＿＿＿＿＿＿＿ Claudia likes *Bret*.
2、＿＿＿＿＿＿＿＿＿＿＿＿＿＿＿＿＿＿＿＿＿ *The boys* found some money.
3、＿＿＿＿＿＿＿＿＿＿＿＿＿＿＿＿＿＿＿＿＿ The girls found *some money*.
4、＿＿＿＿＿＿＿＿＿＿＿＿＿＿＿＿＿＿＿＿＿ My father is *an engineer*.
5、＿＿＿＿＿＿＿＿＿＿＿＿＿＿＿＿＿＿＿＿＿ I sent *my sister* a telegram.
6、＿＿＿＿＿＿＿＿＿＿＿＿＿＿＿＿＿＿＿＿＿ Tomas buys *Serena* three red roses.

7、_____ Is *the woman* at home now?

8、_____ Mr. Jimenez became *a pilot*.

9、_____ He needs *a new car*.

10、_____ Carmen gives them *the books*.

練習問題 1-4

直接目的語として提供された名詞を使って文を書きなさい。

例：the boy

　　Barbara sees **the boy** in the park.「バーバラは公園でその少年を見ている」

1、my sister

_____

2、a new car

_____

3、Jackie

_____

間接目的語として提供された語を使って文を書きなさい。

4、the children

_____

5、a puppy

_____

6、Grandfather

_____

練習問題 1-5

（　　）内の句を用いて、その句を直接または間接目的語として用い、それぞれの疑問文に答えなさい。

　　例：（Yolanda）Whom does Gerry meet?　「ジェリーは誰と会いますか」

　　　　Gerry meets Yolanda.　　　　　　「ジェリーはヨランダと会います」

1. (the boys) Whom does the girl not trust?

_____

2. (his wallet) What does Father often misplace?

_____

3. (the landlord) To whom does she always give the rent money?

_____

4. (her new computer) What does Anita want to sell soon?

_____

5. (her grandchildren) For whom does she buy the toys?

_____

6. (Ms. Johnson) Whom must you visit in New York?

_____

7. (their new house) what do they like so much?

_____

8. (little Johnny) To whom can she give the present?

_____

9. (Dr. Lee) Whom does he need to see today?

_____

10. (Michael) To whom does she throw the ball?

_____

Unit 2｜定冠詞と不定冠詞

英語の定冠詞はtheです。定冠詞は、特定の人や物を明確にするために用います。すでによく知っている誰かそして何かについて話すなら、その名詞にはtheを使いなさい。下の例を見てください。

I already know *the man*	「私はすでにその男を知っています」
She met *the women* who won the lottery.	「彼女は宝くじを当てたその女性たちと会った」
This is *the book* that I told you about.	「これが、私があなたに話した本です」

不定冠詞は、なじみのない、または一般的に話している誰かまたは何かを説明するのに用いられます。不定冠詞には２つの形があります：aとanです。子音字で始まる語の前にはaを、母音字で始まる語の前にはanを用いなさい。それらの例を見てください。

He sees *a stranger* on the corner.	「彼は角の見知らぬ人を見ている」
Did you buy *an apple* or *an orange*?	「リンゴとオレンジのどちらを買いましたか」
Is the woman *a good lawyer*?	「その女性は優秀な弁護士ですか」
She has *an idea*.	「彼女はアイディアを持っている」

それらの文を使って定冠詞と不定冠詞の相違点を比較しなさい。

I want *an* apple. (I do not see an apple. But I feel hungry for one.)
「私はリンゴが欲しい」（リンゴは見えないが、でもリンゴに空腹を感じる）
I want *the* apple. (I am choosing between the apple and the orange that I see before me.)
「私はそのリンゴが欲しい」（目の前に見えるリンゴとオレンジのどちらかを選ぼうとしている）

複数名詞は定冠詞もまたtheです。しかし、複数名詞の不定冠詞はありません。複数形冠詞は単数形冠詞と同じ使用法で用いられます。

練習問題2-1
定冠詞か不定冠詞か、どちらか最もよく意味が通じる方で空欄を埋めなさい。（※問6と8は、回答が２つ考えられる）

1. Did you buy a Ford or _____ Chevy?

2. Does he know _____ man on the corner?

3. She has _____ secret to tell you.

4. What time does _____ train leave?

5. We need _____ hot dogs and a bottle of Coke.

6. Did you see _____ accident?

7. He met _____ guests as they arrived.

8. _____ teacher is angry with us.

9. I can't find _____ keys.

10. Is that _____ snake in that tree?

練習問題2-2
それぞれの文の単数名詞を複数名詞に変更して書き直しなさい。必要な冠詞や動詞に変更を加えなさい。

1. They gave us an orange.

_____

2. I like the book very much.

_____

3. Do you often visit the farm there?

_____

4. A rabbit is hiding behind it.

_____

5. Katrina likes to play with the kitten.

_____

同じ指示に従うが、しかし複数名詞を単数名詞に変更しなさい。

6. Montel has dogs and cats.

_____

7. I want to buy the roses.

_____

8. There are gifts for you.

_____

9. Can you hear the babies crying?

_____

10. Do you have brothers or sisters?

_____

Unit 3 | 形容詞

形容詞は名詞を説明する言葉です。形容詞は、物の大きさ、色、あるいは性質を伝えます：例えば、a *big* room（大きな部屋）、the *red* car（赤い車）、four *interesting* books（4つの興味深い本）。ここに一般的に使用される形容詞がいくつかあります。

beautiful	fast	loud	tall
big	funny	old	terrible
black	handsome	quiet	thirsty
boring	interesting	right	ugly
careful	late	sad	young
careless	little	short	white
early	long	slow	wrong

練習問題3-1

文中でより意味の通じる形容詞を丸で囲みなさい。

1. I often go to a **green/late** movie.

2. Their **little/right** boy is six years old.

3. The **wrong/young** teacher is very smart.

4. We took the **fast/loose** train to New York.

5. The **old /funny** story made me laugh.

6. Do you know that **handsome/early** man?

7. She had an **early/careless** breakfast.

8. I saw the **long/terrible** accident.

9. The new house has **boring/white** doors.

10. The **green/short** boy is my cousin.

名詞と同様に、形容詞は叙述動詞の後に続けることができます。形容詞は、ほとんどの場合、動詞の形がbeあるいはbecomeの後に来ます：

My sister was very *sad*.　　　「私の妹は非常に悲しんでいた」
The horse suddenly became *thirsty*.　　「その馬は突然のどが渇いた」
My grandfather is *old*.　　　「私の祖父は年老いています」

練習問題 3-2

例文を見て、形容詞が叙述動詞の後に続くように、それぞれの文を変更しなさい。

例題：The white house is on the hill.　　「白い家が丘の上にある」
　　　The house on the hill is white.　　「丘の上にある家は白い」

1. The sad song was from Mexico.

_____

2. The funny story is about a clown.

_____

3. The careless waiter is out of work.

_____

4. The ugly snake is from Egypt.

_____

5. The beautiful woman is from Spain.

_____

練習問題 3-3

より分かりやすくさせる形容詞を使って空欄を埋めなさい。Unitの冒頭で与えたリストから選べるかもしれません。

1. David wrote a _____ poem for her.

2. Do you like the _____ cake?

3. I cannot find an _____ book.

4. Where does the _____ lawyer live?

5. Marisa needs a _____ job.

6. The _____ man found a _____ wallet.

7. Kareem is a _____ friend of mine.

8. There is a _____ test tomorrow.

9. When can you come to our _____ farm?

10. That is a _____ question.

Unit 4 人称代名詞

代名詞は名詞の代わりをする語です。英語の人称代名詞は次の通りです：

	単数形	複数形
第1人称	I	we
第2人称	you	you
第3人称	he, she, it	they

注意：youには単数形と複数形の両方があります。1人の人に話しかける時もyouで話し、2人以上の人に話しかける時も、youで話します：

Tim, you are a very good student. 「ティム、君は非常に優秀な学生です」

Bruno and Rene, you have to study more. 「ブルーノとルネ、君たちはもっと勉強しなければなりません」

名詞に性別があるように、代名詞にもまた性別があります。I, we, そしてyouは女性にも男性にも用いることができます。*he*は常に男性に、*she*は常に女性に、そして*it* は常に中性です。3人称の代名詞の複数形は、男性、女性、中性に関わらず常に*they*です。そして名詞と同様に、代名詞も次のように用いることができます：

1、文の主語
2、直接目的語
3、間接目的語

しかし、直接目的語あるいは間接目的語として用いる時、一部の代名詞は変化します：

主語	直接目的語	間接目的語
I	me	me
you	you	you
he	him	him
she	her	her
it	it	it
we	us	us
you（複数形）	you	you
they	them	them

代名詞が文中で名詞にとって代わる場合、代名詞は名詞と同じ特性を持たねばなりません：同

じ数（単数形または複数形）、同じ性（男性、女性、中性）、そして文中で同じ用法（主語、直接目的語、あるいは間接目的語）。代名詞がイタリック体の名詞にとって替わるところを次の例で見てください。

Joseph is a hard worker. → *He* is a hard worker.

「ジョゼフは勤勉家だ」 → 「彼は勤勉家だ」

(singular masculine noun / subject) (singular masculine pronoun / subject)

（「単数形の男性名詞／主語」） （「単数形の男性代名詞／主語」）

Do you know *the girls*? → Do you know *them*?

「あなたはその少女たちを知っていますか」 「あなたはあの人たちを知っていますか」

(plural noun / direct object) (plural pronoun / direct object)

（「複数形名詞／直接目的語」） （「複数形代名詞／直接目的語」）

We gave *Mrs. Jones* some flowers. → We gave *her* some flowers.

「我々はジョーンズさんに花を何本かあげた」 「我々は彼女に花を何本かあげた」

(singular feminine noun/ (singular feminine pronoun/

Indirect object) indirect object)

（「単数形女性名詞／間接目的語」） （「単数形女性代名詞／間接目的語」）

注目：名詞と代名詞は3人称です。これは代名詞が名詞にとり替える時は当てはまります。しかし、名詞または代名詞が1人称単数代名詞Iと組み合わされた場合、それは1人称複数代名詞weに置き換えられます：

You and I have work to do. → *We* have work to do.

「あなたと私はやるべき仕事がある」 「我々はやるべき仕事がある」

He helps *the girls and me*. → He helps *us*.

「彼はその少女と私を手伝う」 「彼は我々を手伝う」

練習問題4-1

（　　　）内に与えられた代名詞を見て、その正しい形を使って文中の空欄を埋めてください。

1.（you）How are _____ today?

2.（he）Caleb gave _____ a gift.

3.（she）_____ lives on Main Street.

4.（it）I really don't like _____ .

5. (I) She met _____ in the city.

6. (Kris and I) Please give _____ the magazines.

7. (you and I) _____ worked in the garden.

8. (they) Are _____ your friends?

9. (we) The puppy followed _____ home.

10. (they) My brother saw _____ in New York.

11. (you) Mikhail wants to visit _____ today.

12. (I) When can _____ move into the apartment?

13. (it) Derrick bought _____ in Mexico.

14. (you and I) The children are helping _____ .

15. (she) I like _____ a lot.

練習問題 4-2

それぞれの文のイタリック体で書かれた名詞を、対応する代名詞に変えなさい。

1. *The students* came to class late. _____

2. I found *the money* in the closed. _____

3. Her brother sent *Jennifer and me* a postcard. _____

4. Do *your parents* live in Florida? _____

5. *My landlady* is very nice. _____

6. Do you know *my landlady*? _____

7. *Boys* can get so dirty. _____

8. Did you lose *your wallet*? _____

9. Juan visits *his uncle* often. _____

10. May I borrow *your watch*? _____

練習問題4-3

それぞれの文のイタリック体で書かれた代名詞を、適切な名詞に変えなさい。

1. *We* often speak English. _____

2. Do you like *it* ? _____

3. Where did you find *them*? _____

4. *She* is from Puerto Rico. _____

5. Patricia never met *him* before. _____

6. *Is he* sick today? _____

7. We sent *them* a box of candy. _____

8. *It* costs twenty dollars. _____

9. The boys watched *her*. _____

10. Do *they* understand us? _____

直接目的語の名詞を直接目的語の代名詞に換える時、間接目的語の名詞あるいは代名詞の前に to あるいは for を加えねばなりません。間接目的語は to あるいは for の前置詞の目的語になります。直接目的語の後に前置詞句を置きなさい。例えば、

    I gave Jay **a book**. → I gave **it** to Jay. 「私はジェイに本を与えた」
    We buy her **flowers**. → We buy **them** for her. 「我々は彼女に花を買います」

練習問題4-4

それぞれの文を、イタリック体で書かれた直接目的語を代名詞に変更し書き直しなさい。その

際、適切なto あるいはfor を加えなさい。

1. I sent my friends *a letter.*

_____

2. She is giving us *two cakes.*

_____

3. They sold her *his car.*

_____

4. I didn't buy Ella *the scarf.*

_____

5. My brother will bring me *my gloves.*

_____

名詞あるいは代名詞は前置詞句を完成させるために用いることができます。それは前置詞そして名詞あるいは代名詞から成り立っている句です。ここに最も一般的に用いられる前置詞のいくつかがあります。

after, behind, between, for, from, in, near, on, of, through, to, with, without,

それらの前置詞句の例を見てください。

after the concert「コンサートの後」　　behind me 「私の後ろ」
between the girls「少女たちの間で」　　for you「あなたのために」
from a friend「友だちから」　　　　　in him「彼の中で」
near the city「街の近く」　　　　　　on it「その上に」
of a book　「本の」　　　　　　　　through her「彼女を通して」
to a student「学生へ」　　　　　　　with us「私たちと一緒に」
without the money「お金なしで」　　　without them「彼らがいなければ」

前置詞句では、直接目的語あるいは間接目的語として用いられているのと同じ形の代名詞を用いなさい。

主格の代名詞	直接あるいは間接目的語	前置詞句
I	me	after me
you	you	behind you
he	him	for him
she	her	from her
it	it	in it
we	us	between us
they	them	near them

練習問題4-5

（　　）内の主格の代名詞を目的格の代名詞に変更して文を完成させなさい。

1. (I) They have a gift for _____ .

2. (you) I sent some flowers to _____ .

3. (he) Karen often comes home without _____ .

4. (she) I like dancing with _____ .

5. (it) We found something in _____ .

6. (we) Teresa sits near _____ .

7. (they) This is a letter from _____ .

8. (Dwayne and I) He is speaking of _____ .

9. (you and I) Someone is standing behind _____ .

10. (he) You can come in after _____ .

練習問題4-6

イタリック体で書かれた名詞を代名詞に変えなさい。

1. We are driving through *the tunnel*. _____

2. A wolf was standing between *the boys*. _____

3. Do you want to ride in *my car*? _____

4. The guests have something for *Julia*. _____

5. I like singing with *Mr. Garcia*. _____

6. Maria is sitting near *Ali and me*. _____

7. I get postcards from *the tourists*. _____

Unit 5 | 動詞

動詞は、文の動作を説明するか、または文の誰かあるいは何かの状況や状態を紹介する文中の言葉です。

動作： 　Anna *throws* the ball. 　　　「アンナはボールを投げる」
条件の紹介：Trent *is* very sick. 　　　「トレントは病状がとても悪い」

多くの動作動詞があります。直接目的語を持つことができるそれらの動詞は、しばしば他動詞と呼ばれます。以下は、一般的に使用される他動詞のいくつかのリストです。注目：他動詞は直接目的語と一緒に用いることができます。

他動詞	文での使用	
buy	He buys a newspaper.	「彼は新聞を買います」
carry	I am carrying the child.	「私は子供を身ごもっています」
find	Can you find the book?	「その本を見つけることができますか」
help	She helps us.	「彼女は我々を助けます」
like	I don't like cabbage.	「私はキャベツが嫌いです」
lose	Don't lose your money.	「お金をなくさないでね」
read	She is reading a book.	「彼女は本を読んでいます」
pull	The dentist pulled the tooth.	「歯医者は歯を抜いた」
push	The boy pushes the cart.	「少年は手押し車を押している」
sell	I am selling my car.	「私は自分の車を売っているところです」
speak	Father speaks Spanish.	「父はスペイン語を話します」
write	We are writing some postcards.	「我々は、はがきを書いています」
understand	Do you understand me?	「あなたは私を理解していますか」

自動詞は、直接目的語を後に続けることができません。自動詞は、しばしば、場所への移動を示し、時には、前置詞句が続きます。下記に一般的に使用されている自動詞のいくつかのリストがあります。

自動詞	文での使用	
come	Can you come to the party?	「パーティーに来てもらえますか」
crawl	The baby crawls on the floor.	「赤ん坊は床を這います」
drive	We are driving fast.	「我々はスピードを出して運転しています」
fly	I flew here from Paris.	「パリからここへ飛行機で来た」
go	Are you going home?	「家に帰るところですか」

hurry	We hurry to the window.	「我々は窓へ急いで行きます」
jump	Peter jumps from the roof.	「ピーターは屋根から飛び降ります」
ride	I am riding in his car.	「私は彼の車に乗っています」
run	The girls run past the school.	「少女たちは学校を走って通り過ぎる」
sail	We are sailing to Europe.	「我々はヨーロッパに向かって航海している」
travel	Do you want to travel with us?	「我々と一緒に旅行しませんか」
walk	I walk out of the theater.	「私は劇場から歩いて出るところです」

なお、他の動詞は、誰かあるいは何かの状況や状態を紹介します。これらの動詞は直接目的語をとれなく、非常に頻繁に形容詞が後に続きます。これらの動詞は、通常、連結動詞と呼ばれます。ここに一般的に使用されるいくつかの連結動詞があります。

連結動詞	文での使用	
appear	The boy appears quite well.	「その少年はかなり元気そうだ」
be	I am hungry.	「お腹がすいている」
become	The weather becomes bad.	「天気は悪くなりそうです」
feel	It feels hot.	「暑く感じる」
grow	The dog is growing weak.	「その犬は次第に衰弱している」
look	She looks unhappy.	「彼女は不幸せそうだ」
seem	The coat seems too small for you.	「そのコートはあなたには小さすぎるように見える」
smell	The pizza smells good.	「ピザはいいにおいがする」
sound	The music sounds awful.	「その音楽はひどい音に聞こえる」
taste	The popcorn tastes salty.	「ポップコーンは塩辛い味がする」

気をつけて下さい！　連結動詞の一部には、もう1つの用法を持つものがあります。それらの動詞は他動詞として用いることもあり得るのです。これらの例を見てください。

　連結動詞：His skin feels *hot*.（*hot* ＝形容詞）「彼の肌は熱く感じる」

　他動詞：He feels *a sharp pain*.（*a sharp pain* ＝直接目的語）
　　　　　「彼は激しい痛みを感じる」

　連結動詞：The sky grows *cloudy*.（*cloudy* ＝形容詞）「空が次第に曇ってきている」

　他動詞：We grow *vegetables*.（*vegetables* ＝直接目的語）「我々は野菜を栽培する」

　連結動詞：That smells *beautiful*.（*beautiful* ＝形容詞）「それはうるわしい香りがする」

　他動詞：She smells the *flowers*.（*flowers* ＝直接目的語）「彼女は花の匂いをかいでいる」

連結動詞：My coffee tastes *bitter.*（*bitter.* ＝形容詞）「私のコーヒーは苦い味がする」
他動詞：Risa tasted *the ice cream.*（*The ice cream* ＝直接目的語）
　　　「リーザはアイスクリームを味見した」

動詞の代わりにam, is, あるいはare を使用すると連絡動詞を識別できます。文が代用語で意味が通じたら連結動詞です。代用語で意味が通じなかったら他動詞です。いくつかの例文があります：

It feels cold.（It *is* cold.）This makes sense.（これは意味が通じる）＝連結動詞
　　「寒気がする（寒い）」
He feels her pulse.（He *is* her pulse.）This makes no sense.（これは意味が通じない）＝
　　他動詞
「彼は彼女の鼓動を感じる（彼は彼女の脈拍である）」

They smell nice.（They are nice.）This makes sense.（これは意味が通じる）＝連結動詞
　　「それらは素晴らしい香りがする（それらはすてきである）」
We smell coffee.（We are coffee.）This makes no sense.（これは意味が通じない）＝他動詞
　　「我々はコーヒーのにおいがする（我々はコーヒーです）」

練習問題5-1
それぞれの文の動詞を見て、それがどんな種類の動詞であるかを決めて、提供された場所に他動詞、自動詞、あるいは連結動詞のいずれかを書きなさい。

1. _____ Kirsten asks a good question.

2. _____ We want to Mexico.

3. _____ Do you understand German?

4. _____ It grows very dark.

5. _____ Emily appears healthy again.

6. _____ Mother bought a new car.

7. _____ The car jumps from the sofa to the chair.

8. _____ Do they want tickets for the movie?

9. _____ The milk is too hot.

10. _____ Grandfather grows corn and potatoes in his garden.

現在時制

一部の言語では、現在時制の活用は非常に複雑です。それぞれの代名詞が、動詞に対し異なる語尾を必要としています。英語はとても単純です。3人称単数形（he, she, it）のみが活用語尾を要求されます。その活用語尾は -s（あるいは -es）です。そしていくつかの動詞に関しては、語尾の変化が全然ありません。現在時制のこれらの例を見てください。

（原形）	go	see	want	can	must
I	go	see	want	can	must
you	go	see	want	can	must
he, she, it	goes	sees	wants	can	must
we	go	see	want	can	must
they	go	see	want	can	must

動詞が母音字 -o で終わる場合、3人称単数形代名詞に対し -es を加えます：

do → does

can と must は特別な助動詞です。それらの助動詞は、現在時制の語尾の変化を全然持っておりません。同じような助動詞は他にもあります。それらは後で取り上げます。

練習問題 5-2
表示された代名詞を使ってそれぞれの文を書き直しなさい。

1. I rarely find a good book.

You _____

He _____

2. We often make mistakes.

She _____

They _____

3. He goes home early.

We _____

I _____

4. It can help us.

   They

   He _____

5. Randy and Kim do the dishes.

   She _____

   You _____

6. I must work tomorrow.

   They _____

   He _____

7. They borrow some money.

   I _____

   She _____

8. He sends a few postcards.

   You _____

   We _____

9. You can spend the night here.

   He _____

   They _____

10. It grows very slowly.

   They _____

   He _____

現在時制で、より複雑な語尾の変化を持つ２つの特別な動詞があります：have と be です。

	have	be
I	have	am
you	have	are
he, she, it	has	is
we	have	are
they	have	are

練習問題5-3

表示された代名詞を使ってそれぞれの文を書き直しなさい。

1. They have no money.

   She _____

   We _____

2. Mario is my cousin.

   He _____

   You _____

3. The boys are very sick.

   I _____

   She _____

4. His father has a new car.

   They _____

   He _____

5. I am at home now.

   They _____

   She _____

6. She is quite well.

   I _____

   He _____

7. He has no tickets.

   They _____

   She _____

8. We have a new apartment.

   You _____

   He _____

9. They are from Costa Rica.

   He _____

   I _____

10. I have a big problem.

They _____

She _____

練習問題5-4

それぞれの文を最良の状態で完成させる太字体の語を丸で囲みなさい。

1. They **goes/have** no time today.

2. My aunt **can/lives** in New York.

3. **She/They** speaks English and Spanish.

4. We **are/am** Americans.

5. **You/It** is in the city.

6. I **must/am** not a citizen.

7. **Are/Have** you at home now?

8. He **has/have** a new job.

9. She **likes/see** her neighbors.

10. **You/ She** goes to the store.

疑問文（質問をする）

be動詞を持つ文は、疑問文を形成するのは容易です。単に動詞と主語の位置を反転させるだけでよいからです。それらの例を見てください。

平叙文	疑問文	
I am late.	Am I late?	「遅れましたか」
She is his sister.	Is she his sister?	「彼女は彼の妹ですか」
They are from Puerto Rico.	Are they from Puerto Rico?	「彼らはプエルトリコ出身ですか」

　haveを含む他の全ての動詞は、do（do, does）動詞を用いることによって疑問文を形成します。do動詞は文の主語に応じて活用されます。文中の本来の動詞は不定詞〈※原形不定詞

と考えてよい〉になります。英語の不定詞は、語toで始まります：例えば、to run, to jump, to sing, など。時々、語toは省略されます：例、run, jump, sing, など。語toは疑問文で省略されます。〈※疑問文や否定文に使われる場合のdoは日本では助動詞と言われている〉

平叙文	疑問文
Jacques has a new job.	Does Jacques have a new job? 　「ジェイクスには新しい仕事がありますか」
You see the ocean.	Do you see the ocean? 　「海が見えますか」
She likes my brother.	Does she like my brother? 　「私の弟を好きですか」
Tanya usually finds the books.	Does Tanya usually find the books? 　「ターニヤは普段本を探して見つけますか」

練習問題5-5

それぞれの文を疑問文に変えなさい。

1. Rocco's uncle lives in Washington.

_____

2. She is his cousin.

_____

3. We take this road to Chicago.

_____

4. They are in the garden.

_____

5. I have your new address.

_____

6. I am your student.

_____

7. Linda likes Jack.

_____

8. You buy flowers every day.

_____

9. She sings beautifully.

_____

10. It is a nice day.

_____

練習問題5-6
それぞれの疑問文を平叙文に変えなさい。

1. Are the boys at home?

_____

2. Do you want this book?

_____

3. Does she have the money?

_____

4. Am I your friend now?

_____

5. Does he go there every day?

_____

6. Is it in there?

_____

7. Do you understand English?

_____

8. Does the boy feel better?

_____

9. Are you in the garden?

---

10. Do we have enough money?

否定（否定文）

　be動詞で否定文を作るには、be動詞の後にnotを加えなさい。

I am	→	I am not
you are	→	you are not
she is	→	she is not
we are	→	we are not
they are	→	they are not

他の全ての動詞に関しては、動詞を否定にするためにはdo / doesとnotを用いなさい。doは文の主語に応じて活用させ、本来の動詞は不定詞になります。その構造は「do + not + 不定詞」です。それらの例を見てください：

本来の文	否定文
I like hot milk.	I do not like hot milk.
	「ホットミルクは嫌いです」
She has my books.	She does not have my books.
	「彼女は私の本を持っていない」
Danielle goes to the window.	Danielle does not go to the window.
	「ダニエルは窓に行かない」
We find the money.	We do not find the money.
	「我々はお金を見つけられない」
It grows cold.	It does not grow cold.
	「寒くならない」

練習問題5-7

それぞれの文にnotを加えて否定文にしなさい。

1. Delores is in the capital.

_____

2. We have enough money now.

_____

3. My father sends him a postcard.

_____

4. The books are on the table.

_____

5. I go home late.

_____

6. I am an American.

_____

7. The girls buy some ice cream.

_____

8. We do our homework.

_____

9. Lisa likes my cousin.

_____

10. It seems very old.

_____

否定文が疑問文になる場合、前に述べたように、その疑問文はdo / doesで始まります。

you do not know　→　do you not know?

Mary does not have　→　does Mary not have?

否定される場合でも、be動詞は、do / does で疑問文を形成しません。

I am not　　　→　am I not?

She is not　　→　is she not?

they are not　→　are they not?

いくつかの例文：

否定文	否定疑問文
She does not like him.	Does she not like him? 「彼女は彼を好きではないのですか」
We do not want it.	Do we not want it? 「我々はそれを欲しくはないのですか」
You are not at home.	Are you not at home? 「あなたは家にいないのですか」
He is not our friend.	Is he not our friend? 「彼は我々の友だちではないのですか」

練習問題 5-8

それぞれの否定文を否定疑問文として書き直しなさい。

1. You do not have the time.

_____

2. Mike does not like this book.

_____

3. Kent is not at home.

_____

4. He does not go there every day.

_____

5. The girls are not happy.

_____

6. Sean does not speak Spanish.

_____

7. The boys do not make a cake for her.

_____

8. They do not have enough money.

_____

9. Mother does not have enough money.

_____

10. I am not happy about it.

_____

現在時制の3つの形式

英語には現在時制を表現するのに3つの方法があります。1つの方法はすでに知っていますね：適切な語尾を加えることで動詞を活用させることです：例えば、I sing, we go, he has, she is, they want, Toni finds. 現在時制のこの構成は、特別な意味を持っています。それは、誰かが習慣としてまたは頻繁に何かを行うことを言うのです。

2つ目の現在時制は、be動詞と語尾が-ingで終わる動詞とを組み合わせて形成されます。：例えば、I am running（私は走っている）, you are speaking, she is learning, we are singing, など。この現在時制の構成は、動作が進行中であり、そして動詞の動作が未完成であることを意味します。〈※［is＋〜ing］この形は、「今まさにしている」の意味で、日本の英文法書では現在進行形と言われる。動作が進行中で未完成の［完結していない］状態と言う意味です〉

3つ目の現在時制は、誰かの供述に対し強調的で反対の応答をすることです。もしその声明が否定的であれば、肯定的な応答を、もし肯定的であれば、否定的な応答です。それは本来の動詞を不定詞にしてdo /doesと用いることを要求します。Kendra say, "You do not have the book." You respond, "I _do_ have the book." Scott say, "He does not go by bus." You respond, "He _does_ go by bus." Sophie say, "My sister likes the movie." You respond, "You sister _does not_ like the movie."

ケンドラは言う、「あなたはその本を持っていないですね」あなたは答える、「いや、私はその本を確かに持っています」スコットは言う、「彼はバスで行かないですね」あなたは答える、「彼は間違いなくバスで行きます」ソフィアは言う、「私の妹は映画が好きです」あなたは答え

る、「妹さんは確か映画が好きでないですよ」

この3つの形を比較してみましょう：

習慣的な供述（頻繁に行われること　）
I speak English.　「私は英語を話します」
We go to school.　「私たちは学校に行きます」
They play soccer.　「彼らはサッカーをします」

進行中で（未完成の）
I am speaking English.　「私は英語を話しています」
We are going to school.　「私たちは学校に行くところです」
They are playing soccer.　「彼らはサッカーをしている」

強意応答
"You do not speak English."　　→　"I do speak English."
「あなたは英語を話せませんね」　「いいえ、私は英語をよく話します」
"We go to school."　　→　"We do not go to school."
「私たちは学校へ行きます」　「いや、私たちは学校へ行きません」
"They do not play soccer."　　→　"They do play soccer."
「彼らはサッカーをしません」　「いいえ、彼らはサッカーをします」

動作が頻繁に行われること示す副詞（often, sometimes, always, usually, every, day, など）を用いる時、現在時制の習慣的な形を用います：例えば、I often listen to jazz. We sometimes talk on the phone. Travis usually works until five. 意味は、「私はしばしば（often）、ジャズを聴きます。私たちは時々（sometimes）電話で話し合いをします。トラビスは通常（usually）5時まで仕事をします」

練習問題5-9
（　　）内の副詞を使ってそれぞれの文を書き直しなさい。その際、動作動詞を未完成のものから習慣的なものに変更してください。

1. We are driving to New York.（always）

_____

2. She is speaking quickly.（sometimes）

_____

3. I am working in the garden. (often)

_____

4. The boys are playing tennis. (frequently)

_____

5. The women are traveling abroad. (every year)

_____

6. Doug is buying German beer. (usually)

_____

7. Michelle is talking on the phone. (always)

_____

8. My brother is sleeping in the living room. (sometimes)

_____

9. They are cooking a roast. (usually)

_____

10. His sister is helping them. (every day)

_____

練習問題 5-10
それぞれの平叙文を強意応答にしなさい。

例：He does not speak English. 　「彼は英語を話せない」
　　He does speak English. 　　「彼は英語をとてもよく話す」

1. She does not understand the problem.

_____

2. We go the movies often.

_____

3. I do not like that dress.

_____

4. Mac wants to sell the old car.

_____

5. Mr. Tyner writes him a long letter.

_____

6. The boys do not work in this factory.

_____

過去時制

過去時制は、過去に起こったことを示すのに用います。現在時制の構成がちょうど3つあるように、過去時制の構成もまた3つあります：（1）習慣的な、または頻繁な動作、（2）進行中で、未完成の動作、そして（3）過去時制の強意応答。

習慣的な、または頻繁な動作の過去時制の活用は、まったく単純です。規則動詞の語尾に -ed を加えるだけです。動詞が -y を従える子音字で終わっていたら、-y を削除して -ied を加えます。1音節の動詞が1子音字で終わっていたら、子音字を重ねて -ed を加えます。これらの例を見てください。

-edを加えるだけ	子音字-y	1子音字
borrow, borrowed	bury, buried	bed, bedded
call,　called	carry, carried	pin, pinned
help,　helped	hurry, hurried	rot, rotted
work,　worked	rally, rallied	sin, sinned

上記に記載された動詞は規則動詞です。規則動詞は -ed を加えることによって過去時制を作ります。また不規則動詞もあります。不規則動詞は動詞の語幹内〈※語尾を除いた残りの部分〉で変化を起こさせ過去時制を形成します。通常は、母音変化ですが、しかし子音変化もまたあり得ます。以下は、いくつかの一般的に使用される動詞の不規則な過去時制の形です：

原形	過去形	原形	過去形
be	was/ were	make	made
break	broke	put	put
bring	brought	read	read
build	built	ride	rode
buy	bought	run	ran

catch	caught	see	saw
cut	cut	sell	sold
do	did	sit	sat
find	found	speak	spoke
fly	flew	stand	stood
go	went	take	took
have	had	teach	taught
hit	hit	throw	threw
lose	lost	write	wrote

付録に不規則な時制の構成リストを掲載しています。

進行中で、あるいは未完成の動作の過去時制を形成するためにはbe（was/were）の過去時制に動詞の語尾を -ing にして加えなさい〈※ ［was/were + 動詞の ~ing］は、日本の英文法書では過去進行形です〉。規則動詞と不規則動詞に違いはありません。

> sing → was singing
> go → was going
> carry → was carrying, など

do（did）の過去時制を用い強意応答の過去時制を形成します。

3つの過去時制の構成を比較してみてください：

習慣的発言（何かが頻繁に行われる）
I spoke English.	「私は英語を話した」
We went to school.	「私たちは学校へ行った」
They played soccer.	「彼らはサッカーをやった」

進行中で（不完全な）
I was speaking English.	「私は英語をずっと話していた」
We were going to school.	「私たちは学校へ行くつもりだった」
They were playing soccer.	「彼らはいつもサッカーをやっていた」

強意応答
"You did not speak English." → "I did speak English."
「あなたは英語を話せなかった」「私は英語をよく話した」
"We went to school." → "We did not go to school."

「私たちは学校へ行った」「私たちは学校へ全く行かなかった」

"They did not play soccer." → "They did play soccer."

「彼らはサッカーをやらなかった」「彼らはサッカーをよくやった」

notを用いた疑問文と否定文は、それらの文が現在時制を形成する場合と同じやり方でdo（did）の過去時制を使って作られます。

現在時制	過去時制
Does he like the article?	Did he like the article?
「彼はその記事が好きですか」	「彼はその記事が好きでしたか」
You do not understand.	You did not understand.
「あなたは理解していない」	「あなたはわからなかった」

練習問題 5-11

それぞれの文を過去時制に書き直しなさい。

1. Susan helps her friends.

_____

2. We go to the movies.

_____

3. She is washing the car.

_____

4. My father is in the kitchen.

_____

5. She does not understand you.

_____

6. Are you satisfied?

_____

7. Do you always speak Spanish?

_____

8. The girls are riding on a horse.

_____

9. He catches the ball.

_____

10. They play chess after supper.

_____

11. Someone has my wallet.

_____

12. Does Mr. Ibrahim live here?

_____

13. They are learning a new language.

_____

14. Karen works in New Orleans.

_____

15. You often make mistakes.

_____

練習問題5-12

習慣的な過去時制を進行中で、不完全な動作の過去時制に変更しなさい。〈※ヒント：使われている動詞を、「be（was・were）＋-ing」形にすればよい〉

例題：I studied it.　　　　　「私はそれを学んだ」

　　　I *was studying* it.　　　「私はそれを学んでいた」

1. He wrote a letter.

_____

2. My mother sat in the garden.

_____

3. Jim stood next to Alicia.

_____

4. The man brought us some fish.

_____

5. We lost the game.

_____

6. The boys hurried home.

_____

7. The dog buried a bone in the yard.

_____

8. I had a bad day.

_____

9. They went to the store.

_____

10. He stayed with an uncle.

_____

練習問題5-13
それぞれの過去時制の文を疑問文に変更しなさい。
〈※2問目のWill［ウィル］は人名〉

1. They made some mistakes.

_____

2. Will played a few games of cards.

_____

3. The girls saw the comet.

_____

4. Her aunt carried the basket into the kitchen.

_____

5. They were in the city all day.

_____

6. Garth learned a good lesson.

_____

7. She was home all day.

_____

8. Robert had the radio.

_____

9. The woman ran for the bus.

_____

10. The dogs fought over a bone.

_____

現在完了時制

過去に始まり現在まで続くものを表現するには現在完了時制を用います。この時制は、2つの構成を持っております：(1) 習慣的な、あるいは頻繁な動作、(2) 進行中で、あるいは未完成の動作。習慣的な現在完了時制は、現在時制のhave（have/has）を活用させ、その活用形と過去分詞を組み合わせて形成されます：

  work → has worked
  carry → has carried
  speak → has spoken

規則動詞の分詞は、過去時制と同じように見えます。過去分詞は-edで終わります。しかし、不規則動詞の分詞は、しばしば変化します。一般的に使用される動詞の不規則分詞の次のリストを見てください。

原形	分詞	原形	分詞
be	been	make	made

break	broken	put	put
bring	brought	read	read
build	built	ride	ridden
buy	bought	run	run
catch	caught	see	seen
cut	cut	sell	sold
do	done	sit	sat
find	found	speak	spoken
fly	flown	stand	stood
go	gone	take	taken
have	had	teach	taught
hit	hit	throw	thrown
lose	lost	write	written

進行中で、あるいは未完成の動作の現在完了形は、have（have/has）を活用させたものとbe（been）の分詞と動詞を -ing で終わらせることによって形成されます。構造は have + been + 動詞 -ing：

work ➔ has been working

carry ➔ has been carrying

speak ➔ has been speaking

この構成では、不規則な分詞について心配する必要はありません。

注目、現在完了時時制が現在時制からどのように形成されるかに注意：

He learns English.
「彼は英語を学ぶ」
He is learning English.
「彼は英語を学んでいる最中だ」
We see strangers.
「我々は見知らぬ人を見る」
We are seeing strangers.
「我々は見知らぬ人を見ている」
I ride a long time.
「私は長い時間乗る」
I am riding a long time
「私は長い時間乗っている」

He has learned English.
「彼は英語を学んだことがある」
He has been learning English.
「彼は英語をずっと学び続けている」
We have seen strangers.
「我々は見知らぬ人を見たことがある」
We have been seeing strangers.
「我々は見知らぬ人をずっと見続けている」
I have ridden a long time.
「私は長い時間乗ったことがある」
I have been riding a long time.
「私は長い時間ずっと乗り続けている」

〈※現在完了形と現在完了進行形の訳文について、上記英文でこの時制に伴う副詞（句）がないため、次のような用法を使って訳文を決めました。

a、現在完了形（have〈has〉＋過去分詞）は、完了（結果）・経験・継続の中から、「（今までに）〜したことがある」の経験で、

b、現在完了進行形（have〈has〉been＋現在分詞）は、「（今まで）ずっと〜し続けている」の過去から現在までの動作の継続で〉

練習問題5-14

習慣的な現在完了時制を、進行中で、未完成の動作の現在完了時制に変更しなさい。

1. Lana has spoken with him.

_____

2. Has he gone to his class?

_____

3. I have worked all day.

_____

4. The tourists have flown around the world.

_____

5. My parents have walked along the river.

_____

6. Has the boy put his toys away?

_____

7. She has taught us all that she knows.

_____

練習問題5-15

現在時制の文を現在完了時制に書き直しなさい。

1. Ms. Nellum takes the boy home.

_____

2. We ride on a bus.

_____

3. They are riding their bikes.

_____

4. Do you often make cookies?

_____

5. She does not understand.

_____

6. They are doing their homework.

_____

7. I am going to the same class.

_____

8. He often breaks his bat.

_____

9. They are breaking windows.

_____

10. Juanita writes her a letter.

_____

練習問題5-16

それぞれの文をより分かりやすく完成させる太字体の語を丸で囲みなさい。

1. Mike has **borrowed/borrowing** my dictionary.

2. We have **been/went** driving all day.

3. **Does/Has** she made fresh bread?

4. Marie **did/has** found your wallet.

5. I have been **listening/listened** to the radio.

6. They have **going/been** home all day.

7. My sister has **going/been** working in the city.

8. **She/They** have taken my money.

9. We have been **hurried/hurrying** to catch the bus.

10. Have you **wrote/written** the postcards?

過去完了時制

過去に始まり過去で終わる動作を表現するには過去完了時制を使用します。過去完了時制には、現在完了時制と同様に2つの構成があります。しかし、過去完了時制では、動詞haveは過去時制（had）で活用されます：

> work → had worked / had been working
> carry → had carried / had been carrying5
> speak → had spoken / had been speaking

動詞と主語を反転させることで現在完了、あるいは過去完了時制の疑問文を形成することができます：

> You have spoken. → Have you spoken?　　「もう、話しましたか」
> He had learned. → Had he learned?　　「学んできましたか」

haveやhadの後にnotを置くことで否定文を形成することができます。

> You have spoken. → You have not spoken.　「話してこなかった」
> He had learned. → He had not learned　　「学んだことがありましたか」

練習問題5-17
現在完了時制の文を過去完了時制に書き直しなさい。

1. Julio has written him a few letters.

_____

50

2. I have been writing a novel.

_____

3. Have you seen a doctor?

_____

4. She has cut her finger.

_____

5. The girls have stayed home again.

_____

練習問題 5-18
現在時制の文を過去完了時制に書き直しなさい。

1. The woman takes the girl home.

_____

2. We ride on a train.

_____

3. I always speak Spanish.

_____

4. Do you often make roast beef?

_____

5. Rebecca does not remember.

_____

6. Is he doing his best?

_____

7. I am going to the movies.

_____

8. Cindy teaches us English.

_____

9. We play the same game.

_____

10. Bethany writes in her diary.

_____

未来時制

未来時制はいくつかの方法で表現することができます。最も一般的なものの1つとして、現在時制を用いることで、未来時制の意味を暗示させることです。これは、進行中で、あるいは未完成の動作に対して現在時制の動詞構成を使用することによってなされます。下記の例文を見てください。

Ray is going to school *today*.（現在時制）	「レイは今日学校に行こうとしている」
Ray is going to school *tomorrow*.（未来時制）	「レイは明日学校に行くつもりだ」
They are traveling to Mexico *today*.（現在時制）	「彼らは今日メキシコに旅立とうとしている」
They are traveling to Mexico *tomorrow*.（未来時制）	「彼らは明日メキシコに旅立とうとしている」

未来時制を形成するもう1つの方法は、動詞〈※日本では助動詞〉shallやwillと不定詞を組み合わせることによってなされます。もし動作が、進行中で、未完成の動作であれば、〈shall / will + be + 動詞の -ing〉の構造を用いなさい：

go → I shall go / I shall be going
speak → he will speak / he will be speaking

それらのそろった活用を見てください。

代名詞	習慣的な動作	未完成の動作
I	shall speak	shall be speaking
you	will try	will be trying
he, she, it	will make	will be making

| we | shall read | shall be reading |
| they | will work | will be working |

伝統的に、shallは1人称単数形と複数形（I and we）に対して使われ続けてきました。しかし、現代の英語の多くの話し手はwillだけを使っています。

動詞と主語を反転させることで未来の疑問文を構成しなさい：

You will sing. → Will you sing?

willの後にnotを置くことで否定文を構成しなさい：

You will sing → You will not sing.

練習問題 5-19

下記の現在時制の文を、willを使った未来時制に書き直しなさい。

1. The girls play soccer.

_____

2. I am learning to drive.

_____

3. We are not home on time.

_____

4. Do you recognize him?

_____

5. Trent is driving to Texas.

_____

6. The men work many hours.

_____

7. She flies to London every year.

_____

8. Dr. Saloff does not treat her asthma.

_____

9. The little boy loses his place.

_____

10. Is he going to the university?

_____

未来完了時制

未来完了時制は、未来時制の始まりと終わりの動作を述べます。他の完了時制と同じように、未来完了時制には、2つの構成があります：1つは、習慣的な、あるいは頻繁な動作に対して、1つは、進行中で、未完成の動作に対してです。習慣的な動作の構造は、〈will ＋ have ＋過去分詞〉です：

       work → will have worked
       see → will have seen

進行中で、あるいは未完成の動作の構造は、〈will ＋ have ＋ been ＋動詞 -ing〉です：

       work → will have been working
       see → will have been seeing

それらのそろった活用を見てください。

代名詞	習慣的な動作	未完成の動作
I	will have spoken	will have been speaking
you	will have tried	will have been trying
he, she, it	will have made	will have been making
we	will have read	will have been reading
they	will have worked	will have been working

練習問題5-20

現在時制の文を未来完了時制に書き直しなさい。

1. My father takes the girl to school.

_____

2. We ride on the subway.

_____

3. They are riding their bikes.

_____

4. Do you make candy?

_____

5. She does not understand.

_____

6. Do they do the work?

_____

7. I am going to the same class.

_____

8. Chet breaks his finger.

_____

9. She arrives by ten.

_____

10. Sabrina writes several notes.

_____

規則動詞と不規則動詞の比較

規則動詞は操作がとても簡単です。活用させても異常な変化をしないので、規則動詞は非常にきちんとしたパターンに従っていると言えます。不規則動詞に関しては、過去時制と分詞が母音の変化によって形成されることを覚えておく必要があります。3つの動詞、そしてそれらの動詞がすべての時制でどのように現れるか見てみましょう。

時制	play	go	sing
現在形	he plays	he goes	he sings
（現在進行形）	he is playing	he is going	he is singing

（強調の現在形）	he does play	he does go	he does sing

過去形	he played	he went	he sang
（過去進行形）	he was playing	he was going	he was singing
（強調の過去形）	he did play	he did go	he did sing
現在完了形	he has played	he has gone	he has sung
現在完了進行形	he has been playing	he has been going	he has been singing
過去完了形	he had playing	he had gone	he had sung
（過去完了進行形）	he had been playing	he had been going	he had been singing
未来形	he will play	he will go	he will sing
（未来進行形）	he will be playing	he will be going	he will be singing
未来完了形	he will have played	he will have gone	he will have sung
未来完了進行形	he will have been playing	he will have been going	he will have been singing

練習問題5-21

下記の現在時制の文を他の5つの時制に書き直しなさい。

1. Sig buys a car.

過去 _____

現在完了 _____

過去完了 _____

未来 _____

未来完了 _____

2. I am helping them.

過去 _____

現在完了 _____

過去完了 _____

未来 _____

未来完了 _____

3. We come home late.

過去 _____

現在完了 _____

過去完了 _____

未来 _____

未来完了 _____

going to と used to は、時制の変化を引き起こす2つの重要な句です。未来時制の shall あるいは

willの代わりに使うものとしてはgoing toを用いなさい。単純過去時制の代わりに使うものとしてはused toを用いなさい。going toあるいはused toと不定詞を組み合わせなさい：

He will learn English. → He is going to learn English.
「彼は英語を学ぶだろう」→「彼は英語を学ぼうとしている」
He spoke English. → He used to speak English.
「彼は英語を話した」→「彼はよく英語を話していたものだった」

未来時制を表すのにbe going toを用いる場合、動作がしようとしていることを暗示しています。単純過去時制を表すのにused toを用いる場合は、動作が習慣で行っていたことを暗示しています。

また、動作がするつもりであったことを表すのに、going toの過去時制（was/were going to）を用いることもできます：

I was going to buy a new car but changed my mind.
「新しい車を買うつもりだったが、気が変わった」
Were you going to visit your aunt?
「あなたは叔母さんをたずねるつもりでしたか」

練習問題 5-22

下記の現在時制の文を、（1）はgoing toを用いた未来時制で（2）はused toを用いた過去時制で書き直しなさい。

1. Bill takes a class at the university.

_____

_____

2. We travel to Germany.

_____

_____

3. I have lots of parties.

_____

_____

4. Do you live in Ecuador?

_____

_____

5. The children watch television every evening.

_____

_____

6. Does she spend a lot of money?

_____

_____

下記の過去時制の文を、過去時制の be going to を使って書き直しなさい。
　　例：I read the novel. 「その小説を読みました」
　　　　I was going to read the novel. 「その小説を読むつもりでした」

7. They sold the old SUV.

_____

_____

8. Liz began her studies at the university.

_____

_____

9. The twins lived together in San Francisco.

_____

_____

10. Did the attorney find a new witness?

_____

_____

Unit 6 | 助動詞

次の3つの助動詞とはすでに遭遇しております：be, do, have。これらの助動詞は活用化させられて、そして動詞の意味や時制を変えるために別の動詞と共に用いられます：

I go　→　I *am* going（進行形であるいは未完成なものに変わった）

you sing　→　*do* you sing?（疑問に変わった）

she makes →　she *has* made（現在完了時制に変わった）

他にも知っておくべき助動詞がいくつかあります。注意：多くの助動詞が、すべての時制で使えるわけではありません。また、場合によっては、特定の時制を形成するために別の動詞〈※日本では助動詞とするものもある〉に変更しなければなりません。下記の例は3人称代名詞 he を使って活用させたものです：〈※日本語の意味は、代表的なもの〉

	be able to（〜できる）	be supposed to（〜することになっている）
現在	is able to	is supposed to
過去	was able to	was supposed to
現在完了	has been able to	has been supposed to
過去完了	had been able to	had been supposed to
未来	will be able to	will be supposed to
未来完了	will have been able to	will have been supposed to

	can（〜できる）	have to（〜しなければならない）
現在	can	has to
過去	could または was able to	had to
現在完了	has been able to	has had to
過去完了	had been able to	had had to
未来	will be able to	will have to
未来完了	will have been able to	will have had to

	may（〜かもしれない）	must（〜しなければならない）
現在	may	must
過去	might	had to
現在完了	該当なし	has had to
過去完了	〃	had had to
未来	〃	will have to
未来完了	〃	will have had to

	ought to（〜すべきである）	should（〜すべきである）
現在	ought to	should
過去	該当なし	該当なし
現在完了	〃	〃
過去完了	〃	〃
未来	〃	〃

	want to（〜したい）	need to（〜する必要がある）
現在	wants	needs to
過去	wanted	needed to
現在完了	has wanted	has needed to
未来	will want	will need to
未来完了	will have wanted	will have needed to

このような助動詞は不定詞〈※動詞の原形〉が後に続きます：

I can go.	I want to go.
You must learn.	You have to learn.
We should help.	We need to help.
He can drive.	He ought to drive.

練習問題6-1

それぞれの文を現在時制で2回書き直してください：1つはcanを追加して、もう1つはwant toを追加してください。

1. Serena buys a new car.

_____

_____

2. We borrow some money.

_____

_____

3. I leave at ten o'clock.

_____

_____

4. The boys have cereal for breakfast.

_____

_____

5. My sister is home by 6:00 P.M.

_____

_____

6. They travel to California.

_____

_____

7. Mr. Gutierrez carries the groceries for her.

_____

_____

練習問題6-2

それぞれの文の助動詞を削除し適切に書き直しなさい。

1. You ought to stay in bed all day.

_____

2. I should try hard.

_____

3. My brother may be a little late.

_____

4. We need to find a room for the night.

_____

5. Ms. Brown is able to get out of bed today.

_____

6. Ramon must remain at home today.

_____

7. They have to learn to behave well.

_____

8. Can you hear me?

_____

9. His girlfriend wants to sell her condo.

_____

10. Do you have to work every day?

_____

動詞と共に一部の助動詞が用いられる時、誰が動詞の動作を実行せねばならないか、その義務がどの程度かを伝えます。下の文を見てください。最初の文は、最小限度の義務を示しています。これは誰も何もする必要のないことです。最後の文は、義務が最大限であることを示しています。これは誰かが絶対にやらなければならないことです。

"We may return the books." (Least obligation. It's our choice.)
「私たちは本を返すことがあります」（最小義務。決めるのは当事者）
"We can return the books." (Little obligation. It's our choice.)
「私たちは本を返すことができます」（少しの義務。決めるのは当事者）
"We are able to return the books." (Little obligation. We have the ability to do this.)
「私たちは本を返すことができます」（少しの義務。当事者はそれを行う能力がある）
"We need to return the books." (Slight obligation.)
「私たちは本を返す必要があります」（わずかな義務）
"We ought to return the books." (Little obligation, but this would be a good idea.)
「私たちは本を返すべきです」（ほとんど義務はないが、それは良い考えでしょう）
"We should return the books." (Little obligation, but this would be a good idea.)
「私たちは本を返すべきだ」（ほとんど義務はないが、それは良い考えでしょう）
"We are supposed to return the books." (Some obligation. Someone has suggested we do this.)
「私たちは本を返すことになっている」（いくらかの義務。誰かが、当事者がこれを行うことを提案している）
"We must return the books." (Greatest obligation. It is our duty to do this.)
「私たちは本を返さなければならない」（最大の義務。当事者はそれをする義務がある）
"We have to return the books." (Greatest obligation. It is our duty to do this.)
「私たちは本を返さなければならない」（最大の義務。当事者はそれをする義務がある）

文に助動詞を加える時、助動詞に対し元来の動詞の時制と同じ時制を使ってください。例えば：“Celeste found（過去時制）a recent biography.「セレステは最近の伝記を見つけた」”の文にhave toを加えた場合、“Celeste had to（過去時制）find a recent biography.「セレステは

最近の伝記を見つけねばならなかった」"と言うように。

練習問題6-3

（　　　）内に提示された助動詞を使って下記の文を書き直しなさい。必ず原文と同じ時制を保持してください。

1. Mr. Weston drives to Arizona.（have to）

_____

2. We borrowed some tools from him.（need to）

_____

3. I left for Mexico on the tenth of May.（want to）

_____

4. Ms. McAdam will help you.（be able to）

_____

5. Jolene repairs the car.（ought to）

_____

6. Did you understand them?（can）

_____

7. Aaron worked on Saturday.（be supposed to）

_____

8. She orders the cake today.（must）

_____

9. Have you filled out the application?（be able to）

_____

10. Our neighbors will paint their house.（want to）

_____

Unit 7 | 受動態

受動態は、文の動作を行ったのが誰であるかを知らなくても供述することができる構造です：
The house was destroyed.（家が破壊された）。または、動作を行った人が文の受動の位置に配置されます：*The house was destroyed by soldiers.*（家は軍人たちによって破壊された）

能動態の文は、一般的に「主語＋動詞＋直接目的語」で構造化されています。受動態の文は、その構造を「主語として直接目的語を用いる＋be＋過去分詞＋by＋前置詞の目的語として主語を用いる」に変えます。2つの構造を比較してみましょう。

能動態の文	受動態の文
Kim finds the dog.	The dog is found by Kim. 「犬はキムに見つけられる」
We buy his car.	His car is bought by us. 「彼の車は我々によって買われる」
The girls stole the purse.	The purse was stolen by the girls. 「財布が少女によって盗まれた」
They solved the problem.	The problem was solved by them. 「その問題は彼らによって解かれた」

受動態のbe動詞は、能動態の動詞と同じ時制で活用されます。さまざまな時制が受動態でどのように現れるか見てください。

時制	受動態の文
現在形	The house is destroyed by the soldiers. 「家は軍人たちによって破壊されている」
過去形	The house was destroyed by the soldiers. 「家は軍人たちによって破壊された」
現在完了形	The house has been destroyed by the soldiers. 「家は軍人たちによって破壊されてきた」
過去完了形	The house had been destroyed by the soldiers. 「家は軍人たちによって破壊されてしまった」
未来形	The house will be destroyed by the soldiers. 「家は軍人たちによって破壊されるだろう」
未来完了形	The house will have been destroyed by the soldiers. 「家は軍人たちによって破壊されているだろう」

現在時制と過去時制だけが、習慣的な活用の形と進行中でまたは未完成の動作に対する活用との間に違いがあります：〈※この点については、Unit 5の現在時制の3つの形式と過去時制の項目を参照願います。現在時制の3つの項目には、現在形と現在進行形が含まれており、過去時制には、過去形と過去進行形が含まれており、その動詞の活用する形に違いがあるということです。進行形の受動態にはbeingが入ります。なお、進行形の受動態は、ぎこちなさがあるため、現在形と過去形以外はほとんど使われません〉

the house is destroyed/the house is being destroyed.
　「家は破壊されている/家は破壊中です」
the house was destroyed/the house was being destroyed.
　「家は破壊された/家は破壊されているところだった」

練習問題7-1
下記の受動態の文を進行形の動作として書き直しなさい。同じ時制を保ちなさい。

1. Glenda is kissed by Stuart.

2. She was spoiled by her parents.

3. My eyes are tested in the clinic.

4. They were arrested for a crime.

5. Monique is awarded a medal.

6. The treasure was buried on an island.

7. The dog is punished again.

8. Was the old barn burned down?

練習問題7-2
下記の受動態の文を現在完了時制に書き直しなさい。

1. We were punished by Father.

_____

2. The man are taken prisoner.

_____

3. She is thanked by happy tourists.

_____

4. I was beaten by a robber.

_____

5. The car was not washed again.

_____

6. Tony is examined by the doctor.

_____

7. They are surrounded by the enemy.

_____

8. Was your sister fired from her job?

_____

9. Was the baby carried to his bedroom?

_____

10. She is congratulated by her boss.

_____

練習問題7-3

下記の能動態の文を受動態の文として書き直しなさい。同じ時制を保ちなさい。

1. A storm destroyed the cottage.

_____

2. Did Columbus discover the New World?

_____

3. They will buy our house.

_____

4. My grandmother has baked the cakes.

_____

5. Phil is cutting the bread.

_____

6. Sergio was selling the newspapers.

_____

7. Has Iris taken the money?

_____

8. She will kiss the baby.

_____

9. Is Max building the fence?

_____

10. Her brother forgot the map.

_____

Unit 8 | 仮定法

仮定法は、いくつか限定されたものですが重要な用法で使われます。仮定法は、要求、提案、要請を表現するのに使われます（*I suggest you be on time.* ＝時間に間に合うよう提案する）；願望を表現するために（If only Jim **were** here. ＝ジムがここにいればなあ）；あるいは、将来の活動への条件を設定するために（We **would leave** if the storm **would let up**. ＝私たちは嵐が和らいだら去るだろう）。これらの使用法を理解するために、仮定法の動詞の活用を調べる必要があります。

現在時制の仮定法〈※仮定法現在〉は、動詞の不定詞から不変化詞の語toを引いて形成されます〈※to不定詞 − to ＝動詞の原形となる〉。注目、それぞれの代名詞は全く同じ動詞の形を必要とします：

代名詞	（原形）be	go	have	work
I	be	go	have	work
you	be	go	have	work
he, she, it	be	go	have	work
we	be	go	have	work
they	be	go	have	work

過去時制の仮定法〈※仮定法過去〉は、規則動詞も不規則動詞もどちらも複数形の過去時制から作られます。注目、それぞれの代名詞は全く同じ動詞の形を必要とします。

代名詞	（過去形）be	go	have	work
I	were	went	had	worked
you	were	went	had	worked
he, she, it	were	went	had	worked
we	were	went	had	worked
they	were	went	had	worked

3番目の仮定法〈※仮定法過去完了〉の動詞の活用は、語wouldに不定詞を加えて形成されます。つまり〈would have ＋過去分詞〉です。それらの例を見てください。

直説法の文	仮定法の文	
He is here.	He would be here.	「仮定法過去」
She buys a book.	She would buy a book.	「仮定法過去」
We have spoken.	We would have spoken.	「仮定法過去完了」

I have played.　　　　　　　　I would have played.　　　　　「仮定法過去完了」

現在時制の仮定法は、要求、提案、要請を表すのに用いられます。この場合、通常の現在時制の活用の代わりに仮定法を用いねばなりません。注目、この場合、接続詞thatを用いるのは任意である。それらの文を検討してください：

She demanded you *be* on time tomorrow. (*are*ではない)
She demanded **that** you *be* on time tomorrow.
「彼女は、明日時間に間に合うようにと要求した」

I suggested he *come* by for a visit. (*comes*ではない)
I suggested **that** he *come* by for a visit.
「彼が訪ねて来るように提案した」

The judge requested the lawyer *have* the documents prepared. (*has*ではない)
The judge requested **that** the lawyer *have* the documents prepared.
「裁判官は弁護士が証拠を準備すべきだと要請した」

これと同じ構造は、他のいくつかの似た動詞でも用いられます：*command, order, propose.*

過去時制の仮定法は、しばしば願望を表すのに用いられます：

I wish Ahmed *were* my brother.　「アフメトがぼくの弟だったらなぁ」
She wished she *had* enough money for a car.
「彼女は車を買うだけの十分なお金があればなあと思っている」
If only my mother *worked* for him, too.
「母がまた、彼のために働いてくれさえすればなあ」
The children wish it already *were* Christmas.
「子供たちは、もうクリスマスであったらなあと思っている」

注目、願望はifあるいはif onlyを文頭で使って表すことができます。

wereは、カジュアルな会話では時には避けるべきであるし、単数形主語では単純過去時制動詞wasによって頻繁に置き換えられていることに気づくべきです（例えば、*I wish Ahmed was my brother.*「アフメトが私の弟だったらいいのに」）。

wouldを用いて形成される仮定法は、文に2つの節があって、その節の1つがif節である場合

に用いられます。この種の文は、1つ目の節で条件を、2つ目の節では動作が起こっていることを設定します。過去時制の仮定法はif節を用います。語wouldはifで始まらない節で出現します。いくつかの例：

If Nadia *were* here, Mother *would be* very happy.
　「もし ナディアがここにいたら、母はとても幸せだろう」
If I *had* a million dollars, I *would buy* a big house.
　「もし億万長者なら、大きな家を買うのだが」
She *would travel* to Spain if her uncle *invited* her.
　「彼女は、叔父が招待してくれれば、スペインへ旅行するだろう」
Mr. Perez *would learn* English if he *lived* in Texas.
　「もしペレス氏が、テキサスに住んでいたら英語を学ぶだろう」

これらの文は、もし条件が適切であったら、現在あるいは将来に起こるだろう動作を表します。

This would happen if these conditions were right.
　「これは、もしこれらの条件が適切であったら起こるだろう」
She *would travel* to Spain if her uncle *invited* her.
　「彼女は、もし叔父が招待してくれればスペインへ旅行するだろう」

同じ形式は、たとえ動詞が現在完了時制のように構成されていても必要とされます。(I have gone, you have seen など)：

If Nadia *had been* here, Mother *would have been* very happy.
　「もしナディアがここにいたら、母はとても幸せだったのに」
Mr. Perez would have learned English if he had lived in Texas.
　「もしペレス氏がテキサスに住んでいたら、英語を学んでいただろう」

これらの文は、条件がすでに適切であったら、過去に起こっていただろう動作を表します。

This would have happened if these conditions had been right.
　「これは、もしこれらの条件が適切であったら起こっていただろう」
Mr. Perez *would have learned* English if he *had lived* in Texas.
　「もしペレス氏がテキサスに住んでいたら、英語を学んでいただろう」

練習問題8-1
（　　　）内の句と直接法の文を組み合わせなさい。その際、現在時制の仮定法に動詞を変更しなさい。

例：（I demand…）He gives me the money.
　　I demand he give me the money. 「彼にお金を支払うよう要求する」

1.（She demands…）Forrest returns home by 5:00 P.M.

_____

2.（The man suggests…）You wear a shirt and tie to work.

_____

3.（They requested…）I am a little more helpful.

_____

4.（My father demanded…）We pay for the damage to the car.

_____

5.（Did he suggest…?）She comes in for an interview.

_____

6.（Roger demands that…）The boy has enough to eat.

_____

7.（Did Mother request that…?）Her will is read aloud.

_____

8.（He has suggested that…）We are trained for other jobs.

_____

9.（Who demanded that…）The statue is erected on this site.

_____

10.（Did he suggest…?）The mayor finds a new assistant.

_____

練習問題8-2
下記のそれぞれの句を適切な文で完成させなさい。

1. He demands _____

2. We suggest _____

3. Dwayne requests _____

4. I must demand that _____

5. Will you suggest to him that _____

練習問題8-3
下記の文を過去時制の仮定法に書き直しなさい。それぞれの文を句 I wish で始めなさい。

1. Becca is here today.

_____

2. We are having a big party for Grandmother.

_____

3. He has enough money to buy a condo.

_____

4. My friends have come for a visit.

_____

5. Darnell doesn't need an operation.

_____

6. His uncle drives slowly.

_____

7. I can borrow some money from you.

_____

8. The weather is not so rainy.

_____

9. They help me every day.

_____

10. She wants to goon vacation with me.

練習問題8-4

下記の句を（　　　）内で提供された文と組み合わせなさい。

　　例：If you were here,…（ I am happy.）

　　　　If you were here, I would be happy.　「あなたがここにいれば、私は幸せだろう」

1. If Evelyn were older, …（ Garrett asks her out.）

---

2. If I had more time, …（ I go to the store.）

---

3. If you spoke louder, …（ He hears you.）

---

4. If it were colder, …（ I turn on the heat.）

---

5. If my brother came along, …（ He helps me wash the car.）

---

6. She would make a cake if…（ It is Erin's birthday.）

---

7. Gary would rent an apartment here if …（ He likes the neighborhood.）

---

8. The boys would play soccer if …（ Someone has a soccer ball.）

---

9. I would speak Spanish if …（ I live in Puerto Rico.）

---

10. The doctor would come to our house if …（The baby is sick.）

練習問題8-5

動詞の現在完了時制を使って下記の文を書き直しなさい。

例：He would buy a car if he had the money.
He would have bought a car if he had had the money.
「もしお金があったら彼は車を買っていただろうに」

1. She would sell me her bicycle if she bought a new one.

_____

2. If you came early you would meet my cousin.

_____

3. If only Karen were here.

_____

4. The children would play in the yard if it were not raining.

_____

5. If the lawyer found the document he would win his case.

_____

6. If only my mother were able to walk again.

_____

7. Juanita would travel to New York if she got the job.

_____

8. If he found the walket he would give it to Rick.

_____

9. Jackie would want to come along if he had more time.

_____

10. If only they understood the problem.

_____

Unit 9 副詞

形容詞が名詞を修飾することはすでに知っていますね。例えば：the *blue* house, our *little* brother, a *silly* poem.　副詞もまた修飾をしますが、しかし、副詞は動詞、形容詞、他の副詞を修飾します。副詞を容易に特定できるのは、語尾がたいてい-lyで終わっているからです：*happily, quickly, slowly, beautifully.*

ほとんどの形容詞は、その末尾に *-ly* を加えることで副詞に変更することができます。形容詞の語尾が *-y* で終わっていたら、*-y* を *-i* に変えて、それに *-ly* を加えます。

形容詞	副詞
bad	badly
bright	brightly
cold	coldly
happy	happily
merry	merrily
speedy	speedily
sudden	suddenly
wrong	wrongly

特別な形や用法を持つ少数の形容詞や副詞があります。重要なものの1つがgoodです。もしgoodが"kind（親切な）"の意味ならば、それは形容詞として使用されるだけです。副詞としてなら、kindの代わりにkindly（親切に）を用いなさい。もしgoodが"talented（有能な）"の意味なら、goodの副詞としてwell（上手に）を用いなさい。注意！　もしwellが"healthy,（健康な）"の意味ならば、それは副詞ではありません；それは形容詞となります。

good = kind：He is a *good* man. 「彼は良い男です」
He spoke to us *kindly*. 「彼は我々に親切に話した」

good = talented：Hayley is a *good* tennis player.
「ヘイリーは優秀なテニス・プレイヤーです」
Hayley plays tennis *well*. 「ヘイリーはテニスがうまい」

well = healthy：I am glad that your father is *well* again.
「あなたのお父さんが、再び健康になれてうれしい」

単語fastは1つの形だけです。fastは形容詞と副詞の両方があります：

Lee is a *fast* talker.　（形容詞）「リーは早口で話す人です」
Lee talks *fast*.　　　（副詞）　「リーは話すのが速い」

そこで注意、副詞 home は語尾が -ly で終わる形はない：

We went *home* after work.　「我々は仕事の後で家に帰った」（home は副詞）

また、文の動詞が特定の質問をすることで、副詞を特定することもできます。how（方法），where（場所），when（時）をたずねなさい。その答えは副詞になります。

How?（方法？）Where?（場所？）When?（時？）	答え＝副詞
Jamal got quickly to his feet.	
「ジャマールはすばやく立ち上がった」	quickly
"How did Jamal get to his feet?"	すばやく
「ジャマールはどう立ち上がったのか」	
She went home on the bus.	
「彼女はバスで家に帰った」	home
"Where did she go on the bus?"	家に
「彼女はバスでどこへ行ったのか」	
They arrived punctually.	
「彼らは時間通りに到着した」	punctually
"When did they arrive?"	時間通りに
「彼らはいつ到着したのですか」	

when の質問に答える時の副詞のいくつかは、語尾が必ずしも -ly で終わるわけではない。
これらの語を検討しなさい：*today, tomorrow, yesterday, tonight, late, early, never.*

しばしば語尾が -ly で終わらない特定の副詞は、形容詞や副詞の意味の程度を制限します：例えば quite, rather, very, somewhat, too：

somewhat slowly = the slowness is not great but evident
　「いくらかゆっくり＝遅さは大きくないが明白だ」
rather slowly = the slowness is emphasized, but it is not extreme
　「かなりゆっくり＝遅さが強調されているが、それは極端ではない」
quite slowly = the slowness is emphasized here

「比較的ゆっくり＝ここでは遅さが強調されている」

very slowly = the slowness is extreme

「非常にゆっくり＝遅さが極端である」

too slowly = the slowness is more than desired

「あまりにもゆっくりすぎる＝遅さが望まれた以上である」

副詞が動詞、形容詞、他の副詞をどのように修飾するか見てみましょう。

動詞	形容詞	副詞
Justin walked *slowly*.「ジャスティンはゆっくり歩いた」	It is an *extremely* strange idea.「それは極端に奇妙なアイディアだ」	She ran *very* fast.「彼女は非常に速く走った」
The boys drove *home*.「少年たちは車で家に帰った」	I have a *very* bad cold.「非常にひどい風邪を引いている」	He sang *too* quietly.「彼はあまりにも静かに歌った」
Hannah laughed *loudly*.「ハンナは大声で笑った」	It was a *rather* stupid question.「それはかなり馬鹿げた質問だ」	I sighed *rather* sadly.「かなり悲しそうにため息をついた」
Carmen writes *carelessly*.「カルメンはいいかげんに書いている」	He was *partially* dressed.「彼は部分的に着飾っていた」	He smiled *quite* cheerfully.「彼はかなり楽しそうにほほえんだ」

練習問題9-1

（　　）内の形容詞を副詞に変更しなさい。その副詞を文中の適切な場所に置きなさい。

1. My sister walked into the room.（timid）

_____

2. We sat down next to the bed.（quiet）

_____

3. Harvey spoke angrily to the man.（rather）

_____

4. The children entered the classroom.（noisy）

_____

5. He said that to the little girl. (too)

_____

6. She talked to the little girl. (harsh)

_____

7. Julia followed the pretty girl. (home)

_____

8. My uncle is a smart man. (very)

_____

9. My cousin plays the piano. (good)

_____

10. The animal stared into my face. (cold)

_____

練習問題9-2
（　　）内の副詞相当語句を使って、適切な文を書きなさい。

1.（very neatly）_____

2.（well）_____

3.（sadly）_____

4.（too）_____

5.（rather quickly）_____

6.（yesterday）_____

7.（never）_____

8.（quite strongly）_____

9.（too carelessly）_____

10.（so beautifully）_____

復習用の練習問題 1

本書のUnit1 ～ 9の内容の力量をチェックするために、下記の練習問題を使用してください。練習の結果に満足できない場合は、適切なUnitを復習して、再度練習を行ってください。

Unit 1
練習問題 R1-1
それぞれの文のイタリック体で書かれた語句を見て、それがどのように使用されているかを決めてください。次に、空欄に主語、直接目的語、間接目的語、前置詞の目的語、あるいは主格補語のいずれかを書きなさい。

1. _____ Mark bought *his grandmother* a dozen yellow roses for her birthday.

2. _____ Will *the tourists* from Greece have any trouble reading the nenu?

3. _____ Maria was writing a story *about him* for her English class.

4. _____ I need to get *a new tire* for my car.

5. _____ We need to decide *what kind of books* to buy for the children.

練習問題 R1-2
（　　）内の語を用いて、指定された形で文を書きなさい。例えば：

（my brother/direct object）＝（私の弟を直接目的語に）　I *gave my brother my old bicycle.*
「弟に古い自転車をあげた」

1. (these people/subject) _____

2. (she/indirect object) _____

3. (the puppies/predicate nominative) _____

4. (we/ direct object) _____

5. (your parents/object of a preposition) _____

Unit 2

練習問題 R1-3

定冠詞か不定冠詞か、どちらかより分かりやすい方で、空欄を埋めなさい。

1. What time does _____ bus arrive?

2. I think I lost _____ directions.

3. Mark found _____ cell phone under a tree in the park.

4. Let's take _____ subway to Central Park.

5. _____ girls and boys participate in many sports.

練習問題 R1-4

イタリック体の名詞が単数形なら、複数形の語を使って文を書き直しなさい。語が複数形なら、単数形の語を使って文を書き直しなさい。

1. The girls like playing with *the puppies*. _____

2. Does John have *a son*.? _____

3. I want to buy *lamb chops*. _____

4. *A raccoon* is hiding under our porch. _____

5. My neighbors gave me *the key* to their house. _____

Unit3

練習問題 R1-5

文中でより分かりやすい方の太字体の形容詞を丸で囲みなさい。

1. Jim needed a **tall / blue / this** shirt for his new suit.

2. The movie we saw was very **sad / regular / handsome**.

3. There was **beautiful / silly / right** sunset last night.

4. Their new apartment has **careful / quick / spacious** rooms.

5. Mr. Garcia's son is quite **long / handsome / annual**.

6. The little girl's behavior is **true / early / terrible**.

7. The **misty / tall / sudden** man is Professor Jones.

練習問題R1-6

より分かりやすくさせる形容詞を使って空欄を埋めなさい。

1. She finally wrote me a _____ letter.

2. Are you wearing my _____ coat?

3. You always ask such _____ questions.

4. That _____ song is about a sailpr who misses his wife.

5. Do you know where her _____ boyfriend lives?

6. They lost their house and have to live in a _____ apartment.

7. This is your _____ story.

8. I seem to have lost my _____ pen.

Unit 4

練習問題R1-7

文をより分かりやすく完成させる太字体の代名詞を丸で囲みなさい。

1. Miguel wanted **you / I / his** to visit him next week.

2. She was crying so we told **her / us / him** a cheerful story.

3. My sister visited **me / I / her** in Miami last week.

4. Is this yours? I found **you / them / it** on the floor.

5. The postcards you sent were beautiful, I loved **your / them / its**.

6. When will **I / them / us** be able to see you again?

7. Please give **you / us / he** a check by tomorrow.

練習問題 R1-8
それぞれの文のイタリック体で書かれた名詞を、対応する代名詞に変更しなさい。

1. *My neighbors* are very friendly. _____

2. *Ms. Lopez* is from Puerto Rico. _____

3. Have you met *John and Maria* yet? _____

4. May I use *your car* for a few hours? _____

5. Laura is anxious to meet *Richard*. _____

6. Juan sent *Jean and me* a book from Portugal. _____

7. *The money* was lying at the bottom of the drawer. _____

8. Do *her brother* work in this office? _____

Unit 5
練習問題 R1-9
イタリック体の動詞が連結動詞、自動詞、他動詞のどれであるか答えなさい。

1. The little boy *ran* into the classroom. _____

2. Why does her forehead *feel* so hot? _____

3. The turkey in the oven *smells* delicious. _____

4. I *tasted* the sour milk and felt ill. _____

5. Can you *speak* a little French? _____

練習問題 R1-10

提供された空欄に、それぞれの動詞の単純過去時制と過去分詞を書きなさい。

例えば、	過去時制	過去分詞
find	found	found
1. go	_____	_____
2. like	_____	_____
3. be	_____	_____
4. give	_____	_____
5. throw	_____	_____

練習問題 R1-11

提供された空欄に、「習慣的な」、「進行中で」あるいは「強調的な」を用いて、句の時制構成を特定しなさい。

1. he is speaking   _____

2. I stood alone   _____

3. she did go home   _____

4. they do the dishes   _____

5. were you working   _____

Unit 6
練習問題 R1-12

（　　）に提供された助動詞を加えてそれぞれの文を変更しなさい。本来の文の時制を維持しなさい。

1. We wash the car every Saturday.（must）_____

2. The children sing sweetly.（to be）_____

3. The patient gets out of bed for a while.（to be able to）_____

4. Bill broke the mirror accidentally.（to have）_____

5. The boys prepare supper tonight.（to be supposed to）_____

6. Have you filled out the application?（to be able to）_____

7. Jean painted her mother's portrait.（to want to）_____

8. Are you funny?（to be）_____

9. We will visit them at Christmas.（to need to）_____

10. My aunt will drive to Los Angeles.（to have to）_____

Unit 7

練習問題R1-13

能動態の文を受動態に書き直しなさい。本来の文の時制を維持しなさい。

1. Mark kisses his grandmother. _____

2. Three men painted the old church white. _____

3. They have arrested three people. _____

4. I will buy a cottage on the lake. _____

5. My uncle is making a delicious soup. _____

練習問題R1-14

（　　）で述べられている時制に受動態の文を書き直しなさい。

1. Several men are forced into the back of the truck.（単純過去）_____

2. Magazines are sold here every day.（現在完了）_____

3. The little girl is spoiled by grandfather.（未来）_____

4. Are the women interrogated?（過去完了）_____

5. His prize mare is awarded the grand prize. （単純過去） _____

Unit 8

練習問題 R1-15

文をより分かりやすく完成させる太字体の動詞の形を丸で囲みなさい。

1. I wish that the rainstorm **ends / would end / end** soon.

2. She would have been so happy if Tom **had been / was / will be** here.

3. I demanded Jack **gives back / return / would send** it to me.

4. Mr. Keller suggests he **was / were / be** more punctual.

5. If Larry **came / come / will come** to the party, we'd have more fun.

6. My uncle requested that his will **is / would / be** read at the memorial.

7. I would bake an apple pie if Mary **were / was / is** back from the Middle East.

8. He wishes they **help / would help / are helping** him scrub the floor.

9. **When / Would / If** Carmen were here, she'd know what to do.

10. Stefan **was / would / were** study with me if I asked.

Unit 9

練習問題 R1-16

提供された空欄に、イタリック体で書かれた副詞の意味を手掛かりにして、how, where, when のいずれかを書きなさい。もし副詞が形容詞または副詞を修飾して機能していたら、修飾語と書きなさい。

1. The children ran *into the family room* to play a video. _____

2. John drove *home* and went straight to bed. _____

3. That was an *extremely* difficult play to understand. _____

4. Her car pulled up to his house *at noon*. _____

5. Laura smiled *warmly* at the handsome man. _____

6. Tom had a *rather* silly look on his face. _____

7. His father had a *very* bad temper. _____

8. Little Jimmy cried *loudly* on the floor. _____

練習問題 R1-17

適切な副詞を使って空欄を埋めなさい。

1. His sister is a _____ smart student.

2. Where did you learn to play the guitar so _____ ?

3. This article is _____ boring.

4. The train _____ arrived.

5. Mr. Brown is a _____ talented artist.

6. She went _____ to bed.

7. With any luck they will get here _____

Unit 10 短縮形

短縮形は、2つの語の組み合わせです。短縮形は、しばしば代名詞と動詞です。ただし、すべての動詞が代名詞と組み合わされて短縮形を作れるわけではありません。これらの動詞〈※助動詞もある〉とだけ用いなさい：have, has, is, are, am, would, will。これらの動詞が代名詞とどのように短縮形を作るか見てください。

代名詞	have / has	is / are / am	would / will
I	I've	I'm	I'd / I'll
you	you've	you're	you'd / you'll
he	he's	he's	he'd / he'll
she	she's	she's	she'd / she'll
it	it's	it's	該当なし
we	we've	we're	we'd / we'll
they	they've	they're	they'd / they'll
who	who's	who's	who'd / who'll

特定の動詞（※　助動詞も含まれている）は否定語notと共に短縮形を作ります。

動詞	短縮
are	aren't
can	can't
could	couldn't
did	didn't
do	don't
does	doesn't
has	hasn't
have	haven't
is	isn't
must	mustn't
need	needn't
should	shouldn't
was	wasn't
were	weren't
will	won't
would	wouldn't

練習問題10-1

それぞれの文の代名詞と動詞を短縮形として書き直しなさい。

1. You have been very unhappy. _____

2. I am not going to work today. _____

3. He would enjoy this movie a lot. _____

4. They are my best friends. _____

5. It is very cold today. _____

6. She will stop by for a visit tomorrow. _____

7. Who has been using my computer? _____

8. He is a very fine teacher. _____

9. We have never seen anything like this. _____

10. I will join you for dinner tomorrow. _____

11. She is a great soccer player. _____

12. Who would want to live in this neighborhood? _____

13. You are spending too much money. _____

14. They have gone to the United States. _____

15. It has been a very humid day. _____

練習問題10-2

それぞれの文の動詞とnotを短縮形として書き直しなさい。

1. You must not act surprised. _____

2. He cannot go to school today. _____

3. Mother will not allow that to happen. _____

4. The boys could not know what danger there was. _____

5. They are not acting properly. _____

6. Did you not do the housework? _____

7. My cousin was not at work today. _____

8. The girls do not like Mark. _____

9. Is that man not your uncle? _____

10. We should not spend so much time together. _____

練習問題 10-3
（　　）に提供された短縮形を使って創意に富んだ文を書きなさい。

1.（hasn't）_____

2.（mustn't）_____

3.（shouldn't）_____

4.（needn't）_____

5.（weren't）_____

6.（I've）_____

7.（he'll）_____

8.（they're）_____

9.（you'd）_____

10.（she's）_____

Unit 11 | 複数形

ほとんどの英語の複数形は、きわめて単純に作られています。名詞の語尾に単に-sを加えるだけです：

    dog → dogs
    building → buildings

ただし、名詞が-s, -ss, -z, x, -ch, -sh, の語尾で終わっていたら、複数形を作るために-esを加えなさい。

    boss → bosses
    box → boxes
    witch → witches
    dish → dishes

名詞が「子音字 + -y」で語尾が終わっていたら、-yを-iに変えて、それから-esを加えます：

    lady → ladies
    penny → pennies

語尾が-oで終わっている語は特別な問題があります。-sを加えて複数形を作るものもあれば、-esを加えて複数形を作るものもあります。これらの例を見てください：

単数形	複数形 + -s	単数形	複数形 + -es
auto	autos	potato	potatoes
piano	pianos	hero	heroes
alto	altos	echo	echoes
zoo	zoos	veto	vetoes
solo	solos	cargo	cargoes

-oで終わる語を用いる複数形の語尾を正確に知るには、辞書を参照してください。

-sで終わる複数形を形成する語がいくつかありますが、しかし、fをvに換える子音字の変更もまた必要です。

    knife → knives

leaf → leaves

shelf → shelves

wife → wives

wolf → wolves

他の特定の名詞は、まったく不規則な方法で複数形を形成します。幸いにも、そのリストはきわめて少ないです。

child → children

mouse → mice

foot → feet

person → people（あるいは persons）

goose → geese

deer → deer（変化なし！）

man → men

woman → women

tooth → teeth

ox → oxen

練習問題11-1

下記の語の複数形を書きなさい。

1. house ＿＿＿＿＿＿＿＿＿＿

2. wife ＿＿＿＿＿＿＿＿＿＿

3. ox ＿＿＿＿＿＿＿＿＿＿

4. fox ＿＿＿＿＿＿＿＿＿＿

5. tooth ＿＿＿＿＿＿＿＿＿＿

6. mouse ＿＿＿＿＿＿＿＿＿＿

7. fez ＿＿＿＿＿＿＿＿＿＿

8. person ＿＿＿＿＿＿＿＿＿＿

9. candy ＿＿＿＿＿＿＿＿＿＿

10. veto ＿＿＿＿＿＿＿＿＿＿

11. deer ＿＿＿＿＿＿＿＿＿＿

12. factory ＿＿＿＿＿＿＿＿＿＿

13. leaf ＿＿＿＿＿＿＿＿＿＿

14. university ＿＿＿＿＿＿＿＿＿＿

15. jury ＿＿＿＿＿＿＿＿＿＿

練習問題11-2

下記の文のそれぞれの名詞を複数形に変更しなさい。必要なら動詞にも変更を加えなさい。

1. The boy is chasing the little mouse.

2. His brother is putting the pot in the box.

_____

3. Does the teacher know the man?

_____

4. The hero of the story was a child.

_____

5. My friend wants to buy the knife, spoon, and dish.

_____

6. A goose is flying over the field.

_____

7. The clumsy person hurt my foot.

_____

8. The poor woman has a broken tooth.

_____

9. We saw a wild ox in the zoo.

_____

10. The ugly witch wanted the trained wolf.

_____

Unit 12 | 句読法

終止符（ピリオド）〔.〕は、文が終わったことを示す一般的に用いられる記号です。ピリオドは2種類の文の後に用いられます：（1）何かについて供述する平叙文、そして（2）依頼や指令をする命令文：

　平叙文：I have five dollars in my pocket.
　　　　　「ポケットに5ドルあります」
　命令文：Give me the five dollars that you have in your pocket.
　　　　　「あなたのポケットにある5ドルを私に下さい」

ピリオドはまた、略語の後にも用いられます。略語にはタイトルとなるものもあれば：Mr., Mrs., Ms., Dr., Rev. のように特定の表現の短い版（バージョン）になるものもあります：A.M., P. M., など。それらの略語の1つを使って文が終わっていたら、2つ目のピリオドは加えないでください。例えば：

　　　　Phillip arrived at exactly 8:00 **P.M.**　「フイリップは午後8時ちょうどに到着した」

文の最後にある疑問符〔?〕は、その文が疑問文であることの記号です。疑問文を形成するために、どのように動詞を配置すべきかについてはすでに知っていますね。いくつかの例：

平叙文	疑問文	
Carlotta is at home.	Is Carlotta at home?	「カルロッタは家にいますか」
You have a problem.	Do you have a problem?	「何か問題がありますか」
They were in Rome.	Were they in Rome?	「彼らはローマにいましたか」

文の最後にある感嘆符〔!〕は、文中の情報が強くまたは感情を込めて述べられていることの記号です。いくつかの普通の平叙文と感嘆文は全く同じように見えますが、しかし、その文が感嘆符で終わっていたら、それは感情をこめて表現されている文です：

普通の平叙文	強い平叙文	
Jason is sick.	Jason is sick!	「ジェイソンは病気なのだ!」
I saw a stranger there.	I saw a stranger there!	「そこで見知らぬ人を見たぞ!」
It has started to snow.	It has started to snow!	「雪が降り始めたぞ!」
He didn't leave.	He didn't leave!	「彼は出発しなかった!」

練習問題12-1

それぞれの文の最後に、ピリオドか、感嘆符か、疑問符か、いずれかを配置しなさい。

1. She took a book from the shelf and began to read _____

2. Do you like living in California _____

3. She asked me if I know her brother _____

4. Sit down and make yourself comfortable _____

5. Shut up _____

6. How many years were you in the army _____

7. I can't believe it's storming again _____

8. When did they arrive _____

9. Watch out _____

10. Her little brother is about eight years old _____

コンマ〔,〕は、文の真ん中でアイディアが分離されていることを示す記号です。これは、アイディアを混乱させないようにするため、あるいはアイディアを区別するためにあるものです。例えば、"When he came in the house was cold.「彼が家には入った時は寒かった」"と"When he came in, the house was cold.「彼が入った時、家は寒かった」"の文を比較してみてください。これは、"He came in the house.「彼は家に入った」"の意味ではない。ここには2つの節の中に2つのアイディアがあるのです。それらがコンマによって分断されているのです：(1) He came in.「彼は家に入った」(2) The house was cold.「家は寒かった」のように。

次の例のような、"He bought pop, tarts, and candy.「彼はポップ、タルト、キャンディを買った」"の文を考えてみましょう。もしpopの後にコンマが省略されていたら、人によっては彼がポップ・タルトを買ったと思うかもしれません。

上記の文では、語andを用いるまでは、すべての項目の後はコンマにすべきです：a boy, a girl, two dogs, and a cat.のような。英語の作家の中には、andの前にコンマを省略することを好む人もおります。

I need paint, brushes, a yardstick, and some tape.
「私はペンキ、ブラッシュ、ヤード尺、そしてテープがいくつか必要だ」
または
I need paint, brushes, a yardstick and some tape.
「私はペンキ、ブラッシュ、ヤード尺といくつかのテープが必要だ」

コンマはまた、命令または質問の対象となる人の名前を区切るためにも用いられます：

Janelle, call Mr. Montoya on the telephone.
「ジャネル、モントーヤ氏を電話で呼び出してくれませんか」
Dr. Gillespie, will my husband be all right?　「ガレスピー博士、夫は大丈夫ですか」
Boys, try to be a little quieter.　「君たち、少し静かにしようよ」

コンマはまた、名詞を修飾する2つ以上の形容詞を分離するのにしばしば必要とされます：

She wore a red, woolen jacket.　「彼女は赤い、ウールのジャケットを着ていた」
The tall, muscular man was a weightlifter.
「背の高い、筋肉隆々の男は重量挙げの選手だった」

重文として結びつけられている2つの独立節を分離するためにはコンマを用いるべきです。重文は、頻繁に次の接続詞で結びつけられます：and, but, for, not, or, so, yet. のような。独立節は、主語と述語を持ち、それが単独になった場合でも、意味が通じるものです。いくつかの例：

DeWitt is baking a cake, and Allison is preparing the roast.
「デウィットはケーキを焼いている。そしてアリソンはローストを準備している」
Do you want to go to a movie, or should we just stay home?
「映画を見に行きたいですか、それとも単に私たちと家にいた方が良かったですか」
It began to rain hard, yet they continued on the hike.
「雨が激しく降り始めたが、彼らはまだハイキングを続けていた」

感嘆符と一般的な表現は、コンマで文の残りの部分から分離すべきです：

Oh, I can't believe you said that!
「ええっ、あなたがそんなことを言ったなんて信じられないわ」
No, I don't live in Germany anymore.　「いえ、もうドイツに住んでいません」
Yes, you can go outside now.　「ええ、すぐに外へ出られます」

Well, you really look beautiful tonight.
「ところで、あなたは今夜、本当にすばらしく見えるわ」
By the way, my mother is coming for a visit.
「話の途中ですが、母が泊まりに来ているんですよ」

コンマは、日付から曜日を、年から月日を分離する場合に必要です。月や年のみが指定されている場合、コンマは省略されます。

He arrived here on Monday, June 1st. 「彼は 6 月 1 日、月曜日にここに到着した」
My birthday is January 8, 1989. 「私の誕生日は、1989 年の 1 月 8 日です」
The war ended in May 1945. 「戦争は 1945 年 5 月に終わった」

少数点〔.〕は、ピリオドのように見えます。一部の言語では、少数点はコンマで区切られます：6,25 あるいは 95,75. しかしアメリカ英語では、少数点はピリオドで区切られます：6.25 あるいは 95.75.

大きな数値では、英語では千の位がコンマで区切られます。他の言語では、それらはピリオドか、あるいはスペースを空けることによってしばしば分割されます：

英語の数	他の言語の数
1,550,600	1.550.600 あるいは 1 550 600
22,000,000	22.000.000 あるいは 22 000 000

練習問題 12-2
それぞれの文を書き直し、必要な場所にコンマを置きなさい。

1. Ms. Muti please have a seat in my office.

_____

2. She bought chicken ham bread and butter.

_____

3. By the way your mother called about an houre ago.

_____

4. Paul was born on May 2 1989 and Caroline was born on June 5 1989.

_____

5. No you may not go to the movies with Rich!

---

6. Well that was an interesting discussion.

---

7. The men sat on one side and the women sat on the other.

---

8. Oh the dress hat and gloves look beautiful on you Jane.

---

9. It happened on April 5 1999.

---

10. Yes I have a suitcase and flight bag with me.

コロン〔：〕は、物事のリストまたは特別な関連情報が続くことの記号です。例えば：

You'll need certain tools for this project: a hammer, screwdriver, hacksaw, and chisel.
「このプロジェクトのため特定の道具を必要とするでしょう：例えば、ハンマー、ドライバー、弓のこ、のみ」
I suddenly understood the plot of the story: A man steals a thousand dollars to help his dying son.
「突然、物語の筋書きを理解した。つまり、ある男が死にかけている息子を助けるために千ドル盗むのです」

コロンはまた、時刻を伝える時、分から時間を分離するのに使われます：5:30, 6:25 A.M.,11:45 P.M.

セミコロン〔；〕は、コンマとピリオドの両方によく似ている句読点です。セミコロンは、アイディアの間に一時停止があること、そしてそれらのアイディアが密接につながれていることの記号です。セミコロンは、2つの関連した独立節を1つの文にしばしば結び付けることがあります：

Jamal is a powerful runner; he is determined to win race today.

「ジャマールは強力なランナーです；彼は今日のレースで勝つことを決意している」

Loud music filled the room; everyone was dancing as if entranced.

「大音量の音楽が部屋にあふれていた；誰もがまるでうっとりとなって踊っていた」

練習問題12-3

空欄に、コロンかセミコロンかどちらかを配置しなさい。

1. There are some things you need for this recipe _____ sugar, salt, and flour.

2. She understood the meaning of the story _____ Thou shalt not kill.

3. Peter is an excellent swimmer _____ he coaches a team at our pool.

4. This document is important _____ it will prove his innocence.

5. Add these names to the list _____ Irena, Helen, Jaime, and Grace.

引用符〔""〕は、誰かが言った言葉を囲い込みます。引用符は、直接引用を示します。直接引用と間接引用との違いを見てください。

直接引用文	間接引用文
He said, "Stay where you are."	He said that I should stay where I am.
「彼は、"あなたがいるところに留まっていて"と言った」	「彼は、私がいるところに留まるべきだと言った」
She asked, "Is that Tran's brother?"	She asked if that is Tran's brother.
「彼女は "あれがトランの弟ですか" とたずねた」	「彼女は、あれがトランの弟かどうかとたずねた」

引用されている文に属するすべての句読点は、引用符の内側に囲い込まれることを覚えておいてください。

正しい：He asked, "Does she often visit you?" 「彼は、"彼女はあなたをしばしば訪ねるのですか" とたずねた」

間違い：He asked, "Does she often visit you"?

短編小説または雑誌の記事のタイトルは、引用符で囲い込むべきです：*"My Life on a Farm" by James Smith*. が、もし引用語句が引用文の内側に置かれていたとしたら、それは単一引用符によって囲い込まれるべきです：このように、*He said, "I just read, ' My life on a Farm' by*

James Smith." 彼は言った、"ジェイムズ・スミスによる"「農場での私の生活」を今ちょうど読んでいる、と。

練習問題12-4
それぞれの文を書き直し、必要なところに引用符を追加しなさい。

1. She asked, Why do you spend so much money?

_____

2. I learned that from Tips for Dining Out in a restaurant magazine.

_____

3. Rafael said, Elena's grandfather is very ill.

_____

4. This is going to be a big problem, he said sadly.

_____

5. Kurt will say, I already read The Ransom of Red Chief in school.

_____

アポストロフィー〔'〕が、短縮形を作る際に用いられることはすでに知っていますね。

  I am → I'm
  we are → we're

アポストロフィーは、また所有格を作るのにも用いられます。単数形名詞が所有の意味を作るためには、-'sを加えます。-sで終わる複数形名詞の場合は、アポストロフィーを加えるだけです。他のすべての複数形は-'sで終わります。

名詞	所有格の形	意味
boy	the boy's dog	the dog that belongs to the boy 「少年の犬」
boys	the boys' games	the games that belong to the boys 「少年たちが所属しているところの試合」
house	the house's roof	the roof of the house 「家の屋根」

Tom	Tom's aunt	an aunt of Tom's 「トムの叔母」
book	a book's pages	the pages of a book 「本のページ」
men	the men's work	the work that the men do 「男性がする仕事」

もし語が-sで終わる場合、その語の発音が所有格で別の音節を必要とする場合、所有格を作るために-'sを加えることができます：

Lois → Lois's
Thomas → Thomas's
actress → actress's

別の音節が所有格を作るのに発音されない場合、アポストロフィーだけを加えなさい；これは複数形の場合にありがちなことです：

actresses → actresses'
railing → railings'
classes → classes'

短縮形の複数形を作るためにアポストロフィーを使用するのはよくあることです：*two Dr.'s*,（2年先生）、*three M.D.'s*,（3年医師）*four Ph. D.s'*.（4年博士号医師）。同じことは数や文字の複数形を作る時にも該当します："You had better mind your p's and q's.「あなたは言動に注意した方がよい」

練習問題12-5
それぞれの文の書き直し、必要な場所にアポストロフィーを追加しなさい。

1. The geeses eggs are well hidden.

_____

2. She cant understand you.

_____

3. Is Mr. Hancocks daughter still in college?

_____

4. The two girls performance was very bad.

_____

5. Ms. Yonans aunt still lives in Mexico.

_____

6. She met several M.D.s at the party.

_____

7. Do you know Mr. Richards?

_____

8. The womens purses were all stolen.

_____

9. He wont join the other Ph.D.s in their discussion.

_____

10. It isnt right to take another mans possessions.

_____

練習問題 12-6
空欄に、欠けている句読点の形を書きなさい。

1. Blake _____ will you please try to understand my problem?

2. They went to England _____ Wales, and Scotland.

3. Someone stole my money _____

4. She asked, _____ When is the train supposed to arrive?"

5. Mr. Wilson _____ s son wants to buy a house in Wisconsin.

6. I have the following documents _____ a will, a passport, and a visa.

7. Grandmother died September 11 _____ 1999.

8. Jack is a pilot _____ he flies around the world.

9. Well _____ I can't believe you came home on time.

10. Are you planning another vacation _____

Unit 13 | 不定詞と動名詞

すでに不定詞と、それらが動詞としてどのように使われているかに気づいていますね。しかし、不定詞は他の方法でもまた用いることができます。

不定詞は名詞としても用いることができる：*To run would be cowardly.*
「走るとは卑怯だろう」（文の主語）
不定詞は副詞としても用いることができる：*We came here to thank you.*
「私たちはあなたに感謝したいためにここに来た」（私たちが来た理由）
不定詞は形容詞として用いることができる：*He is the man to trust.*
「彼は信頼できる人です」（man を修飾）

動名詞は、現在分詞に似ています：動詞に -ing 語尾（ running, looking, buying, など）を加えます。しかし、動名詞は現在分詞とは違います。現在分詞は、進行中で、未完成の動作を形成するのに用いられます：*I was running, she is speaking, they are helping.*「私は走っていた。彼女は話している。彼らは手伝っている」。 そして分詞として現在分詞は形容詞で用いることができます。しかし、動名詞は名詞として用いられます。それらの例を見てみましょう。

現在分詞	動名詞
She was baking cookies.	Baking takes a lot of time.
「彼女はクッキーを焼いていた」	「パンを焼くのは時間がかかる」
I am living alone.	I don't like living alone.
「私は一人暮らしをしている」	「私は、一人暮らしは好きではない」
We have been relaxing at home.	Relaxing will help relieve the tension.
「私たちは家でずっとくつろいでいる」	「くつろぐことは緊張を取り除く助けになる」
He was spelling the new words.	Spelling is my best subject.
「彼は新しい言葉を綴っていた」	「綴り方は私の得意科目です」

練習問題13-1
それぞれの文を見て、不定詞がどのように用いられているか決めなさい。そして、提供された空欄に名詞、副詞、形容詞のいずれかを書きなさい。

1. _____ I bought the car *to make* you happy.

2. _____ He doesn't like *to run* after a big dinner.

3. _____ The book *to read* is Moby Dick.

4. _____ She gave me a gift to show her gratitude.

5. _____ To pay taxes is a privilege.

練習問題 13-2
それぞれの文を見て、イタリック体で書かれた語がどのように用いられているか決めなさい。
そして、提供された空欄に、動詞、形容詞、名詞のいずれかを書きなさい。

1. _____ *Running* water is a modern convenience.

2. _____ We are *taking* the family on a picnic.

3. _____ This is a *continuing* problem.

4. _____ *Playing* in the street is dangerous.

5. _____ I don't like *skiing*.

6. _____ Do you prefer *jogging* or tennis?

7. _____ The *laughing* clown was very funny.

8. _____ We've been *driving* all day.

9. _____ The *beginning* of the story was quite sad.

10. _____ He was arrested for *speeding*.

Unit 14 | 関係代名詞

関係代名詞は、2つの文で同じ名詞や代名詞を持っている場合、2つの文を結びつけるのに用います。関係代名詞は、関係節の先頭部分を形成します。英語には、5つの基本的な関係代名詞の形があります：

> that ＝有生名詞あるいは無生名詞のいずれかに言及する時に用いる
>
> who ＝有生名詞に言及する時に用いる
>
> which ＝無生名詞に言及する時に用いる
>
> whose ＝所有格として用いる
>
> 関係代名詞の省略＝関係代名詞が省略された時に発生する

導入節〈※　関係詞に導かれる節〉の名詞は先行詞と呼ばれます。関係代名詞は、2番目の節（関係詞節）で名詞に置き換えられます。

関係代名詞が2つの文をどのように結びつけるか見てみましょう。同じ名詞または代名詞が両方の文で見つかったら、2番目の文は、関係代名詞を省略できるし置き換えもできます。次に、2つの文を1つの文として述べます。注目、有生名詞または無生名詞が関係代名詞でどのように変化するか。

> 2つの文：He likes *the girl*. *The girl* comes from Alaska.
>
> 関係詞節：He likes the girl **who** *comes from Alaska*.　または
>
> He likes the girl **that** *comes from Alaska*.
>
> 「彼が好きな少女はアラスカ出身です」

> 2つの文：I bought *the car*. *The car* needs repairs.
>
> 関係詞節：I bought the car **that** *needs repairs*.　または
>
> I bought the car **which** *needs repairs*.
>
> 「私は車を買ったが、その車は修理する必要がある」

名詞は、主語、直接目的語、間接目的語、前置詞の目的語、そして所有格として使用することができます；だからまた、それらの語を置き換えて関係代名詞にもできます。

that, who, whichには特別な用法があります：ただし、カジュアルな会話では、関係代名詞が所有格を示す場合を除いて、関係代名詞thatは、whoまたはwhichの代わりに用いることができます。無生名詞を使ったそれらの例を見てください。

文中の用法	一対の文	関係詞節を形成
主語	I found the money. The *money* was lost.	I found the money that was lost. I found the money which was lost. 「失くしたお金を見つけた」
直接目的語	I found the money. Bree lost the *money*.	I found the money that Bree lost. I found the money which Bree lost 「ブリーが失くしたお金を見つけた」
間接目的語	該当なし	該当なし
前置詞	I found the money. They spoke *about the money*.	I found the money that they spoke about. I found the money about which they spoke. 「彼らが話していたお金を見つけた」
所有（格）	I found the money. The color *of* the money is green.	I found the money the color of which is green. 「緑色のお金を見つけた」

無生物の目的語では、whose を of で始まる前置詞句の代わりに用いることは可能です：*I found the money whose color is green.*（= I found the money the color of which is green.)

ところで、有生名詞を使った類似した例を見てください：

文中の用法	一対の文	関係詞節を形成
主語	I found the boy. The *boy* was lost.	I found the boy that was lost. I found the boy who was lost. 「道に迷っていた少年を見つけた」
直接目的語	I found the boy. Kim met the *boy*.	I found the boy that Kim met. I found the boy whom Kim met. 「キムが出会った少年を見つけた」
間接目的語	I found the boy. They gave the *boy* a gift.	I found the boy that they gave a gift to. I found the boy to whom they gave a gift. 「彼らが贈り物を与えた少年を見つけた」
前置詞	I found the boy. They spoke *about the boy*.	I found the boy that they spoke about.

I found the boy about whom they spoke.

「彼らが話していた少年を見つけた」

所有（格）　I found the boy. The *boy's* father is a soldier.

I found the boy whose father is a soldier.

「父が軍人である少年を見つけた」

気をつけて下さい！　もしwhomやwhichが前置詞句の一部であったら、前置詞はwhomやwhichの前に置くことができますし、あるいは関係詞節の最後に置くこともできます：

I like the man *for whom* I work.

I like the man *whom* I work for.

「私は仕事をしている男が好きです」

These are the books *about which* she spoke.

These are the books *which* she spoke *about*.

「彼女が話していた本があります」

関係代名詞がthatである場合、前置詞は常に関係詞節の最後に置かれます：

I like the man *that* I work *for*.

These are the books *that* she spoke *about*.

間接目的語の名詞が関係代名詞に変更される場合、前置詞toあるいはforは原文の意味を伝えるために追加されるべきです。いくつかの例：

Do you know the man? I gave the man ten dollars.

Do you know the man *to whom* I gave ten dollars?

「私が10ドル与えた男を知っていますか」

Andre saw the girl. I bought the girl some flowers.

Andre saw the girl *that* I bought some flowers *for*.

「アンドレは私が花を買ってあげた少女を見た」

関係代名詞が直接目的語あるいは前置詞の目的語として使われた場合、その関係代名詞は省略できます。その時、関係代名詞の省略と呼ばれます。前置詞が関わっていたら、その前置詞は関係詞節の最後に置かねばなりません。

用法	関係代名詞の使用	省略された関係代名詞
直接目的語	He's the man that I met in Canada.	He's the man I met in Canada.
前置詞	Where's the car in which she was sitting?	Where's the car she was sitting in?

「彼は私がカナダで会った男です」

「彼女が座っていた車はどこですか」

注目：カジュアルな会話では、多くの英語の話し手が規則的にwhoをwhomに置き換えていることに気づくべきです。

関係詞節には2種類あります：制限節と非制限節です。制限的な関係詞節〈※ 限定用法とも言う〉は、文の意味上、欠かせない情報を含んでおります。もしその情報が省略されれば、文が意図したものが理解されないかもしれません。制限的な関係詞節は、他の節で話題に上がった人あるいは物を特定します。ここに2つの例を示します：

The woman who stole the ring was soon arrested. (*who stole the ring is* essential information)

「指輪を盗んだ夫人がすぐに逮捕された」（指輪を盗んだ人は、必要不可欠な情報である）

What's the make of the car that you bought? (*that you bought* is essential information)

「あなたが買った車の車種は何ですか」（あなたが買った車は、必要不可欠な情報）

非制限的な関係詞節〈※ 継続用法とも言う〉は、単に追加情報を伝えるが、しかし、他の節で話題に上がった人や物について明確にするものではありません。関係代名詞thatは、非制限的な関係詞節で用いるべきではありません。しかし、カジュアルな会話では、しばしばthatと関係代名詞whoとwhichとの間で置き換えがあります。ここに非制限用法の2つの例を示します：

The mayor, who is out of town right now, will give a speech on Friday. (*who is out of town right now* is additional but nonessential information)

「ただ今、市長が市外にいるので、金曜日に演説を行うでしょう」（ただ今、市長は町から離れているのでは追加であって、必ずしも必要な情報ではない）

The play, which lasted over three hours, was given rave reviews. (*which lasted over three hours* is additional but nonessential information)

「3時間以上続いたこの劇は、称賛されました」（3時間以上続いた劇は追加であって、必ずしも必要な情報ではない）。

コンマは、文中で他の節から非制限的な関係詞節を分離するのに用いられます。

練習問題14-1

2番目の文を関係節に変更して下記の文を結び付つけなさい。関係代名詞としてthatを用いなさい。

1. I found the money. The money belonged to Jack.

_____

2. She has a good memory. Her memory always serves her well.

_____

3. This is the woman. I told you about the woman.

_____

4. I have a document. The document proves my innocence.

_____

5. They want to visit the country. Marsha comes from the country.

_____

上記と同じやり方に従い、関係代名詞としてwho, whom, whose,を用いなさい。

6. This is the doctor. The doctor saved my life.

_____

7. Do you know the musician? I met the musician in Hawaii.

_____

8. She likes the gentleman. I was telling her about the gentleman.

_____

9. I visited the sisters. The sisters' father had recently died.

_____

10. Jerod noticed the stranger. All the neighbors were staring at the stranger.

_____

上記と同じやり方に従い、関係代名詞としてwhichを用いなさい。

11. Pablo threw away the picture. The boys had found the picture.

_____

12. I live in the house. My grandfather was born in the house.

_____

13. He bought a suit. The suit is navy blue.

_____

14. Anna has a new hat. I like the new hat very much.

_____

15. He wanted to paint the bench. A man was sitting on the bench.

_____

練習問題14-2
適切な節を使ってそれぞれの文を完成させなさい。

1. This is the lady about whom _____

2. We visited a country that _____

3. I don't like the people whom _____

4. Where's the basket in which _____ ?

5. Peter laughed at the story that _____

6. My aunt met the writer whom _____ about.

7. Sammie spoke with the teacher whose _____

8. I met the manager whom _____ for.

9. She hates the blouse that _____

10. Tell me about the tourists whose _____

練習問題 14-3

関係節をその省略形に変更して、関係代名詞を省略し、それぞれの文を書き直しなさい。

　　例：She's the girl whom I met there. 「彼女は私がそこで会った少女です」
　　She's the girl I met there.

1. He was in the city that I visited last year.

_____

2. Did you finally meet the woman about whom I was telling you?

_____

3. Ron sold the house that he was born in.

_____

4. My father lost the checkbook that he kept his credit card in.

_____

5. Did you find the ball that I threw over the fence?

_____

6. That's the pretty girl for whom I wrote this poem.

_____

7. I don't know the people whom he gave the flowers to.

_____

8. The hat from which the magician pulled a white rabbit was empty.

_____

9. She forgot the tickets that she had placed next to her briefcase.

_____

10. They live in a tiny village, which we finally located on a map.

_____

Unit 15 | 再帰代名詞

再帰代名詞は、文の主語に戻って反映させます。英語の再帰代名詞は次のようなものがなります：*myself, yourself, himself, herself, itself, ourselves, themselves.* それぞれの再帰代名詞は、その人称代名詞が文の主語である場合にのみ、その人称代名詞の対応物と共に用いることができます：

人称代名詞	再帰代名詞	見本文
I	myself	I hurt myself again.「またけがをした」
you	yourself	You can do it yourself.「自分自身でそれをやることができる」
he	himself	He enjoyed himself.「彼は楽しく過ごした」
she	herself	She helped herself to some candy.「彼女はキャンディを自由に取って食べた」
it	itself	It destroyed itself in a few seconds.「それは数秒で自分自身を破壊した」
we	ourselves	We found ourselves in a strange city.「気がついたら私たちは見知らぬ都市にいた」
you	yourselves	You must clean yourselves up before dinner.「あなたは夕食前に身なりを整えなければならない」
they	themselves	They accidentally burned themselves.「彼らはうっかりしてやけどをした」

もし再帰代名詞と人称代名詞に対応物がなければ、その時には、人称代名詞が文中で用いられるべきです。それらの例を見てください：

対応物	対応物がない
I hurt myself again.「またけがをした」	I hurt him again. I hurt them again.「また彼を傷つけた」「私は彼らをまた傷つけた」
He enjoyed himself.「彼は楽しく過ごした」	He enjoyed it. He enjoyed them.「彼はそれを楽しんだ」「彼はそれらを楽しんだ」
They harmed themselves.「彼らは自分自身を傷つけた」	They harmed me. They harmed her.「彼らは私を傷づけた」「彼らは彼女を傷づけた」

３人称単数形と複数形の名詞は、適切な３人称単数形と複数形の再帰代名詞に用いることを覚

えてください。

Marta bought herself a new car.　　　　「マルタは自分用に新しい車を買った」
The boy cut himself.　　　　　　　　　「少年はけがをした」
The alien creature wounded itself with its own claws.
　　　　　　　　　　　　　「エイリアンは自分自身の爪でけがをした」
The men helped themselves to some beer.　「男たちは自由にビールを取って飲んだ」

練習問題 15-1

提供された主格の人称代名詞を使って、それぞれの文を適切に書き直しなさい。適切な再帰代
名詞に変更しなさい。

1. I found myself in a difficult situation.　「気がついたら困難な立場にいた」

You（単数）_____

He _____

She _____

We _____

They _____

Amy _____

2. We enjoyed ourselves at the party.　「私たちはパーティーで楽しく過ごした」

I _____

You（複数）_____

He _____

She _____

They _____

The boys _____

3. He is going to be very proud of himself. 「彼は自分をとても誇りに思うでしょう」

I _____

My friends _____

Mother _____

They _____

We _____

Abdul and Ricky _____

4. I just couldn't help myself. 「私はまさにどうしようもなかった」

You（複数）_____

He _____

She _____

We _____

They _____

The men _____

練習問題 15-2
それぞれ文の目的格の人称代名詞を、適切な再帰代名詞を使って置き換えなさい。

1. Jerry liked me in the new suit.

_____

2. They busied her with several different tasks.

_____

116

3. We were very proud of them.

_____

4. She is buying us a few new outfits.

_____

5. The children hurt me.

_____

6. I have to ask him what to do now.

_____

7. The young woman told you not to give wera.

_____

8. He wants to find me something nice to wear.

_____

9. You've harmed no one but us.

_____

10. The lizard hid them under a rock.

_____

Unit 16 | 所有格

名詞は２つの方法で所有格を形成します：（1）前置詞ofの目的語になる、あるいは（2）語尾に -'s（-sにアポストロフィーをプラスする）を加える。
それらの例を見てください：

the roar of a lion	a lion's roar　「ライオンの咆哮」
the color of the book	the book's color　「本の色」
the children of Mrs. Diaz	Mrs. Diaz's children　「ディアス夫人の子供たち」
the prey of the wolves	the wolves' prey　「オオカミの獲物」

（アポストロフィーを使用するための規則を確認するには、句読法に関するUnit12を参照してください）

所有格は、何かが誰にあるいは何に所属するかを示すために用います：

This is *Ginny's* car.　　　　　「それはジニーの車です」
The kittens *of an alley cat* have a hard life.
　　　　　　　　　　「路地裏の子猫はつらい生活を送っています」

練習問題16-1
イタリック体で書かれた所有格の句を -'sで終わる所有格に変更しなさい。
　　例：The color of the car is red.　「車の色は赤い」
　　　　The car's color is red.

1. The center *of the storm* was just north of the city.

_____

2. The condition *of the victims* was very serious.

_____

3. I don't understand the behavior *of my classmates*.

_____

4. The equipment *of the lab* was outdated.

_____

5. The efforts *of each man* helped to make the project a success.

6. The many illnesses *of the animals* were evidence of the filthy conditions.

7. The documents *of the young lawyer* were very impressive.

8. The room was filled with the scent *of the roses*.

9. A hunter captured the mother *of the little bear cub*.

10. We drove to the northern border *of the town*.

Unit 17 | 所有代名詞

所有代名詞は、時々、所有形容詞とも呼ばれます。所有代名詞を何と呼ぼうとも、その用法は明快で単純です。あたかも再帰代名詞のように、所有代名詞にも、人称代名詞の対応物があります。その関係を確認するために所有代名詞の一覧表を見てください。

主語	目的語	所有代名詞１	所有代名詞２
I	me	my	mine
you	you	your	yours
he	him	his	his
she	her	her	hers
it	it	its	its
we	us	our	ours
they	them	their	theirs

所有代名詞の１と２の用法には相違点があります。所有代名詞１は、常に名詞の前に置かれ名詞を修飾します。所有代名詞２は、名詞が理解されると、所有代名詞１と名詞に置き換わります。それらの例を見てください。

My gift is unusual.

「私の贈り物は珍しいものです」

Is this *your* brother?

「こちらはあなたの弟さんですか」

Our friends live here.

「私たちの友だちがここに住んでいる」

His aunt is a doctor.

「彼の叔母は医者です」

Her dress is very nice.

「彼女のドレスはすてきです」

Which gift is *mine*?（my gift）

「どちらの贈り物が私のものですか」

The seat on the right will be *yours*.（your seat）

「右側の席があなたの席でしょう」

These two dogs are *ours*.（our dogs）

「これら２匹の犬は私たちのものです」

His is a doctor.（his aunt）

「彼の叔母は医者です」

Hers is very nice.（her dress）

「彼女のドレスはすてきです」

所有代名詞は、ものが誰にあるいは何に所属しているかを伝えます。

練習問題17-1

所有代名詞の１を所有代名詞の２に変更して名詞を省略しなさい。

例：She has my book.　　「彼女は私の本を持っている」

　　She has mine.　　「彼女は私の本を持っている」

120

1. The car on the corner is my car.

_____

2. Was this your house?

_____

3. The invading soldiers searched their house.

_____

4. Did Dee find her briefcase?

_____

5. Our relatives have lived in Brazil for a long time.

_____

6. His boss is fair with everyone.

_____

7. These problems are entirely his problems.

_____

8. I need your advice.

_____

9. My landlord is going to raise the rent.

_____

10. Their long conversations made no sense.

_____

練習問題　17－2

イタリック体で書かれた語句を文の主語の所有代名詞の対応物に変更しなさい。

　例：He likes _the_ new car.　　「彼は新しい車が好きです」

　　　He likes his new car.　　「彼は自分の新しい車が好きです」

1. The women want to visit _some_ relatives in Europe.

_____

2. She takes *the* children for a long walk.

_____

3. Do you have *the* tools in the truck?

_____

4. I sent *the* address and telephone number to the office.

_____

5. We want *this one*.

_____

6. The picture fell out of *the* frame.

_____

7. They spend a lot *of* time in Canada.

_____

8. Are you selling *these*?

_____

9. I left some papers in *the* apartment.

_____

10. Jose found *the* wallet under the red.

_____

練習問題 17-3
それぞれの文をより分かりやすく完成させる太字体の語を、丸で囲みなさい。

1. Did you leave **your / mine / your** keys on the desk?

2. Her brother met **his / her / their** wife in Paris.

3. This book is **our / his / her,** and that one belongs to Smita.

4. Where did they buy **theirs / blouse / its**?

5. I believe I forgot **mine / my / its** again.

6. My sister gave **mine / her / its** watch to me.

7. I saw your tickets, but where are **her / my / ours**?

8. **Hers / Theirs / His** uncle is coming to America to live.

9. The fox hurt **its / hers / front** foot in a trap.

10. May I have **hers / my / mine** dinner now?

Unit 18 | 前置詞

前置詞は、文中で特定の語を名詞あるいは代名詞に結びつけます。しかし、前置詞句（前置詞が名詞や代名詞を後に従える）の意味はさまざまです。前置詞句は、どこで（where）、いつ（when）、なぜ（why）、どのように（how）、だれの（whose）を伝えます。それらの例を見てください：

where（場所）	= in the garden	「庭の中」
when（時）	= until Monday	「月曜日まで」
why（理由）	= because of the bad weather	「悪天候のために」
how（方法）	= by train	「列車で」
whose（所有）	= of the bride	「花嫁の」

一般的に使用される前置詞のいくつかのリストを次に示します。

about	behind	for	since
above	below	from	through
across	beside	in	to
after	between	of	under
along	by	off	until
around	despite	on	up
at	down	out	with
before	during	over	without

複合前置詞（あるいは群前置詞）は複数の語から成り立っています：along with, because of, due to, in spite of, on account, next to, on top of, together with, など。

名詞が前置詞句内で用いられる時、名詞は変化しませんが、しかし、たいていの代名詞は変化します：

I → with me	we → from us
you → to you	they → for them
he → by him	the boys → to the boys
she → without her	a girl → after a girl
it → on it	my keys → over my keys

練習問題18-1

前置詞句の名詞句を適切な代名詞に変更しなさい。同じ数と性を保持しなさい。

1. The man next to Jordan is a senator.

_____

2. Did they leave after the play?

_____

3. Evan was dancing with his aunt.

_____

4. Why did you leave the house without your wallet?

_____

5. Are there washers and dryers in the apartments?

_____

6. Juan had some nice wine for his guests.

_____

7. The man with Yvette is her new boyfriend.

_____

8. A large bear was coming toward the man.

_____

9. The letter from my parents made me very happy.

_____

10. In spite of all her problems, Tonya went on smiling.

_____

注目：文の主語に接続する前置詞句は、時には混乱を引き起こすことがあります。それらの要素の一方が単数形で他方が複数形である場合、とりわけ当てはまります。前置詞句ではなく、主語が動詞の形を決定することを常に覚えておいてください。

単数形主語＋前置詞の複数形目的語

The box of fresh cookies *was* torn open by their dog.

　「新鮮なクッキーの箱がそれらの犬によって引き裂かれ開けられた」

〈※ The box ＝単数形主語、of fresh cookies ＝前置詞の複数形目的語、動詞 was ＝単数形〉

Each of you *has* a duty to help them.

　「あなた方それぞれは彼らを助ける義務がある」

〈※ each は原則として単数扱いのため動詞は単数形の has〉

One of the youngest candidates *needs* a lot more money.

　「立候補者の中で最も若いものは、より多くのお金を必要とする」

複数形主語＋前置詞の単数形目的語

The musicians in the little band *were* given a new contract.

　「小さな楽団の音楽家たちは新しい契約を交わされた」

〈※ The musicians ＝複数形主語のため動詞は複数形 were〉

Several girls from our school *have* been awarded scholarships.

　「私たちの学校から幾人かの少女たちが奨学金を授与されてきた」

練習問題18-2

それぞれの文をより分かりやすく完成させる太字体の語を、丸で囲みなさい。

1. One of the boys **are / is / were** a friend of mine.

2. The **woman / person / women** from our church are having a bake sale.

3. Each of the people at these meetings **want / have to / needs** to know the truth.

4. The box of chocolates **was / are / were** a gift from Thomas.

5. The students in this class **need / wants / has** more time to prepare.

6. Every one of you on the team **want / has / have** the chance to be a champion.

7. The magician, together with his assistants, **makes / are making /make** the rabbits disappear.

8. All of you in the third row **needs / need / was needed** to stand up.

9. Many tourists on this flight **doesn't / don't / does** have the proper visa.

10. a young teacher, along with several of her pupils, **find / are locating / captures** the robber.

Unit 19 | 大文字使用

名詞が、固有名詞と普通名詞の2つの一般的な部門に分類されることはすでに知っていますね。すべての名詞は、人、場所、ものごと、アイディアに言及しますが、しかし、特定の名詞、つまり固有名詞のみが大文字で書き始めます。他のすべての名詞は大文字で書く必要はありません（それらの名詞が文頭にある場合を除いて）。英語の大文字使用を統制している詳細を見てください。

A. 文の最初の語は常に大文字で書き始めます。文が普通名詞または他の文法的要素で始まっているかどうかには関係ありません。

Terrell is my brother.	「テレルは私の弟です」
The children are fast asleep.	「子供たちは熟睡中です」
Are you going home now?	「今から帰るところなの」
When is that program on?	「そのプログラムはいつ作動しますか」

B. どんな芸述作品（例えば、短編小説、論文、本、TV番組、映画、絵画作品、歌、CD）でもタイトルの最初の語は、常に大文字で始めます。タイトルの他のすべての語も大文字で始めます。ただし論文、接続詞、前置詞は除きます（しかし、論文、接続詞、前置詞がタイトルの最後の語である場合は、大文字にすべきです）。

"How to Buy a House"	「家の買い方」（本のタイトルの一部）
The Adventures of Tom Sawyer	「トム・ソーヤーの冒険」（本のタイトル）
Finding Nemo	「ファインディング・ニモ」（映画のタイトル）
"Take Me Out to the Ball Game"	「私を野球に連れてって」（歌のタイトル）

C. 同じ規則が企業や機関の正式名称にも適用されます。

The University of Illinois at Chicago	「イリノイ大学シカゴ校」
Sears Roebuck and Company	「シアーズローバックアンドカンパニー」

D. ファーストネーム（名前）、ラストネーム（姓）、イニシャル、個人的な肩書などは常に大文字で書き始めます。

Jason Kensington	「ジェイソン・ケンジントン」
Ms. Alicia Jones	「アリシア・ジョーンズさん」
Professor Rosa Morena	「ロサ・モレナ教授」

Senator William Hayes	「ウィリアム・ヘイズ上院議員」
General Dwight D. Eisenhower	「ドワイト・D・アイゼンハワー将軍」
J.D. Powers	「J・D・パワーズ社」

E.　肩書を持っている人に直接宛てた部分の一部でない肩書は、大文字にしないでください。下記のものを比較してみてください。

I met a senator at the meeting.	Hello, Senator. How are you?
「私はその会議で上院議員と会った」	「こんにちは、上院議員、お元気ですか」
Is she the governor now?	It's good to see you, Governor Bejcek.
「彼女は今知事ですか」	「会えてうれしいわ、ベジャク知事」
A captain entered the room.	Please sit down, Captain Bligh.
「艦長が部屋に入った」	「どうぞお座りください、ブライ艦長」

F.　すべての曜日、すべての月、そして休日は大文字で書き始めます。季節やその他の時間の部分は大文字にしなくてもよいです。

Is it Monday already?	The weather is cooler in the fall.
「もう月曜日ですか」	「天候は秋の寒さだ」
My favorite month is June.	Where do you spend the winter?
「私の大好きな月は6月です」	「冬はどこで過ごしますか」
She was born March 3, 2001.	How many years are in a decade?
「彼女は2001年3月3日に生まれた」	「10年で何年になりますか」
Today is the Fourth of July.	The twentieth century was important.
「今日は7月4日です」（米国独立記念日）	「20世紀は重要だった」
I like Halloween.	It's a new millennium.
「ハロウィーンが好きです」	「新千年紀だ」

G.　時間の略語には特別な規則があります。B.C.とA.D.は常に大文字で書き始めます。B.C.はキリスト以前に起こった時代と年に用います。A.D.はキリスト紀元（主の年）に起こった時代と年に用います。つまり、キリスト誕生後の最初の年から始まります（B.C.は日付に続きます；A.D.は日付に先行します）。A.M.とP.M.は大文字にする場合としない場合があります。A.M.は真夜中から正午までの時間を指し、P.M.は正午から真夜中までの時間を指します。

That happened in the fifth century B.C.	「それは紀元前5世紀に起こった」
Columbus first landed in the New world in A.D.1492.	
「コロンブスは西暦1492年に初めて新世界に上陸した」	
They arrived exactly at 9:00 P.M.	「彼らはちょうど午後9時に到着した」

I set my alarm for 7:35 A.M. 「目覚ましを7時35分に設定した」

練習問題19-1
大文字を必要とするそれぞれの文の語をいくつか書き直しなさい。

1. john bought a new cadillac for his wife.

_____

2. is colonel brubaker a friend of governor dassoff?

_____

3. the president of the company was born on march tenth in the city of buffalo.

_____

4. we stopped at a restaurant in chicago and ordered southern fried chicken.

_____

5. in the summer the kids from whittier school play baseball at st. james park.

_____

6. she invested some money last february with e. f. hutton in new york.

_____

7. ms. assad met the general while he was touring the northern part of texas.

_____

8. are mr. and mrs. cermak planning a large wedding for their daughter, britney?

_____

9. red bought us a cole and a hot dog for lunch.

_____

10. the students read *the adventures of huckleberry finn* in school iast may.

_____

11. his sister was born on may tenth in cleveland memorial hospital.

_____

12. mia got up a precisely right O'clock a.m.

_____

13. do you know the president of the corporation?

_____

14. if you see mayor yamamoto, tell him the governor has phoned again.

_____

15. we get the new york times every day but Sunday.

_____

練習問題 19-2

下記の日付を語として表示されている数字で書き直しなさい。数字の順序は月 / 日 / 年に対応しています。

1. 5/10/1865 _____

2. 11/11/1918 _____

3. 7/4/1776 _____

4. 12/24/2000 _____

5. 1/1/1999 _____

語として下記の時間を書き直しA.M.またはP.M.を加えなさい。どちらに決めるかを助けるために（　）内の句を見てください。

6. 9：00（in the morning）_____

7. 12：30（in the evening）_____

8. 6：45（at dawn）_____

9. 7：50（at sunset）_____

10. 8：15（during breakfast）_____

復習用の練習問題2

本書のUnit10 ～ 17の内容の力量をチェックするために、下記の練習問題を使用してください。
練習の結果に満足できない場合は、適切なUnitを復習して、再度練習を行ってください。

Unit 10
練習問題R2-1
提供された語句を組み合わせて短縮形を作りなさい。

1. he is not _____

2. we would _____

3. they have _____

4. I should not _____

5. who has _____

6. it is _____

7. we were _____

8. he does not _____

9. I am _____

10. she will _____

Unit 11
もし太字体の名詞が単数形なら、複数形に変更しなさい。もし太字体の名詞が複数形なら、単数形に変更しなさい。

1. The **factory** is old. _____

2. He chased the little **mouse**. _____

3. His **feet** are big. _____

4. Where is your **brother**? _____

5. The **wife** sits on the sofa. _____

6. The **leaves** are falling already. _____

7. I met the **women** in Toronto. _____

8. Did he use a **veto**? _____

9. I found the sharp **knives**. _____

10. Did they find the old **ox**? _____

Unit 12

練習問題 R2-3

文を正確に完成させる句読点は何ですか。

1. Mr. Johnson _____ please have a seat _____

2. Watch out _____ You're in danger _____

3. How old is your grandmother _____

4. _____ This is going to be problem _____ "he said.

5. The man _____ s name is Thomas _____

6. I have the evidence _____ it will prove his innocence _____

7. Add these to your grocery list _____ milk _____ eggs _____ and bread.

8. Bob asked, _____ Where is the bank _____ "

9. Well _____ you came home on time today _____

10. He spoke with an M.D _____ at one.

Unit 13
練習問題 R2-4

不定詞あるいは動名詞のどちらが文を適切に完成させるか、（　）内の動詞を言い換えなさい。

1. （make）I quit smoking _____ you happy.

2. （read）The best book _____ is *Catcher in the Rye*.

3. （live）I don't enjoy _____ in this building.

4. （get）He was arrested for _____ drunk.

5. （bore）This is a very _____ film.

6. （show）Tom sent me a check _____ his appreciation.

7. （hike）Do they really like _____ ?

8. （end）The _____ was so sad that I cried.

9. （visit）The store _____ is Macy's.

10. （chirp）The _____ birds sound so happy.

Unit 14
練習問題 R2-5

2つの文を組み合わせて、2番目の文を、代名詞thatを使った関係節にしなさい。

1. This is the jacket. The jacket belonged to Maria. _____

2. What is the country ? Max came from the country? _____

3. Did you meet the woman? I met the woman in Madrid. _____

4. I found the money. He hid the money in the attic. _____

who あるいは which の形で2つの文を組み合わせなさい。

5. He learned another language. It is a difficult task. _____

6. Where's the box? I put the books in the box. _____

7. I spoke with the boy. His sister is a police officer. _____

関係代名詞で省略して文を言い換えなさい。

8. This is the gentleman, to whom I gave my passport. _____

9. Is that the hat, in which he carried the message ? _____

10. That's the girl that I really like. _____

Unit 15
練習問題 R2-6
提供された新しい主語を使ってそれぞれの文を言い換えなさい。

He really enjoyed himself.
1. I _____

2. She _____

3. They _____

提供された新しい主語で書きそれぞれの文を言い換えなさい。

He was happy with himself.
4. You _____

5. We _____

6. Who _____ ?

7. The twins _____

136

提供された新しい主語でそれぞれの文を言い換えなさい。

He couldn't help himself.

8. I _____

9. Tina _____

10. John and Mike _____

Unit 16

練習問題R2-7

ofを使って形成された所有格を、'sまたはs'で形成された所有格に文を言い換えなさい。

1. The health of the woman was good.　　　　_____

2. The end of the storm was a relief.　　　　_____

3. The buzzing of the bees scares her.　　　　_____

4. Are the pups of the German shepherd healthy?　　　　_____

5. I don't like the behavior of that child.　　　　_____

練習問題R2-8

'sまたはs'で形成された所有格を、ofで形成された所有格に言い換えなさい。

1. The boys' shouting disturbed him.　　　　_____

2. Are those elks the lion's prey?　　　　_____

3. The town's western border is Main Street.　　　　_____

4. The victim's condition grew worse.　　　　_____

5. Where are the doctor's instruments?　　　　_____

練習問題 R2-9

太字体の名詞を省略し、適切な文に言い換えなさい。

1. Is the car down the street your **car**?   _____

2. Tom wanted my **keys**.   _____

3. **His sister** danced with everyone.   _____

4. **The snake's** nest was behind a rock.   _____

5. Jane found our **computer** in the basement.   _____

練習問題 R2-10

太字体の語を適切な所有代名詞に変更しなさい。

1. John took **the** dog for a walk.   _____

2. The photograph slipped put of **the** frame.   _____

3. **Some** students made Mr. Connlly proud.   _____

4. I rarely spend **a lot of** time sleeping.   _____

5. Will you visit **some** friends in Washington?   _____

Unit 20 | 比較級と最上級の形

形容詞あるいは副詞の比較級は、ある人またはものと別の人やものとの比較を述べます。ほとんどの比較級では、語尾に -er を必要とします。例えば、taller, shallower のように。形容詞あるいは副詞が、単一の子音字で終わる場合、その子音字を末尾（-er）に加える前にダブらせます。例えば、mad → madder. のように。形容詞や副詞が、語尾が-y で終わっていたら、-y を -i に変えて-er を加えます。例えば、funny → funnier のように。

形容詞や副詞の最上級は、形容詞や副詞の意味するものの程度が最も高いことを示します。たいていの最上級は、語尾が-est で終わります。例えば、tallest, shallowest のように。形容詞あるいは副詞が、単一の子音字で終わっていたら、その子音字を語尾に加える前にダブらせます。mad → maddest のように。形容詞や副詞が、語尾が-y で終わっていたら、-y を -i に変えてから -est を加えます。funny → funniest のように。

比較級と最上級の両方とも、more や most を用いることによって別の方法で形成させます。more という語は、比較級を形成するために形容詞や副詞の前に置かれ、そして most という語は、最上級を形成するために形容詞や副詞の前に置かれます。例えば、more interesting / most interesting, more logical / most logical のように。この構成は、主に、２音節以上の語、あるいはフランス語、ラテン語、または他の外国を根源とするものから英語に来た語に用いられます。

その他の構成（ long, longer, longest）は、アングロサクソンを起源とします。比較級と最上級のこれらのリストを比べて見てください。

アングロサクソンを起源		外国語を起源	
bigger	biggest	more critical	most critical
finer	finest	more dangerous	most dangerous
grander	grandest	more dynamic	most dynamic
happier	happiest	more fruitful	most fruitful
jollier	jolliest	more harmonious	most harmonious
kinder	kindest	more hopeless	most hopeless
mightier	mightiest	more intense	most intense
poorer	poorest	more sensitive	most sensitive
smaller	smallest	more visible	most visible
thinner	thinnest	more willing	most willing

注目：-ful, -less, -ing で終わる語は、比較級と最上級を形成するのに more と most を用います

が、だからと言って、それらの語は、外国語を起源とするものではありません。

不規則に構成されるいくつかの語は、単純に記憶しなければなりません：

原級	比較級	最上級
bad	worse	worst
far	farther / further	farthest / furthest
good	better	best
little	less	least
many	more	most
much	more	most
well	better	best

ある人やものが、比較されるべき別の人やものに言及することなく、文中で比較級を使用することは可能です。これらの例を見てください：

Jorge is a lot *taller*. 　　　　　　　　「ジョージは相当背が高い」
My sister was *thinner* a few years ago. 　「妹は数年前かなりやせていた」

このような文では、比較される人やものが想定されます。人やものが、比較されるべき別の人やものを述べる時は、than という語を用いてください：

Jorge is a lot taller *than* Michelle. 　　「ジョージはミシェルより背が高い」
My sister was thinner a few years ago *than* she is now.
　　　　　　　　　　　　　　　　　　　「妹は、数年前は今よりやせていた」

比較級での形容詞と副詞の両方の構成はまったく同じです。相違点は、それらが文でどのように使用されるかです：

My car is faster than your car.（形容詞）　「私の車はあなたの車より速い」
She runs faster than you do.（副詞）　　　「彼女はあなたより速く走る」

語尾が -ly で終わる副詞では、比較級と最上級の両方の形が可能です：

He spoke *quicker*. / He spoke *more quickly*.
「彼はより早く話した」/「彼はより早く話した」
He spoke the quickest. / He spoke *the most quickly*.
「彼は話すのが一番速かった」/「彼は最も早く話した」

最上級の形容詞と副詞はしばしば、theという語によって先行されます：

Lars is *the* strongest boy.　　　　　「ラーズは最強の少年です」

She is *the* most beautiful girl here.　「彼女はこの辺で最も美しい少女です」

最上級が叙述形容詞である時、名詞が後に続かない上に、語theは省略され得ます〈※叙述形容詞とは、単独で補語になれる形容詞〉：

Lars is strongest when he's not tired.　「ラーズは疲れていない時、最強です」

She is most beautiful when she wakes up in the morning.

「彼女は朝起きた時、最も美しいです」

more と most で形成されている比較級と最上級の副詞は、副詞的な語尾 -ly を必要とします。

more willingly　　　「もっと喜んで」

most capably　　　「最も見事に」

練習問題20-1

イタリック体で書かれた語を比較級に変更して、それぞれの文を書き直しなさい。

1. This freight train is moving *slowly.*

_____

2. My *young* brother is a mathematician.

_____

3. Where is the *old* man you told me about?

_____

4. Fanny swims *well*, but she still cannot dive.

_____

5. Hunter's cold is *bad* today.

_____

6. They have *much* to do before the end of the day.

_____

7. I think Robbie is *intelligent*.

_____

8. The new employee is *careless* about his work.

_____

9. She has *many* friends in the city.

_____

10. This project is *critical* to the success of the company.

_____

11. Clarice just can't speak *quietly*.

_____

12. We have a *big* house out in the country.

_____

13. Do you think that kind of language is *sinful*?

_____

14. The inn is *far* down this road.

_____

15. Your friend is *reckless*.

_____

練習問題20-2
文を書くために、語それぞれの一式を用いなさい。thanを使って比較級を作りなさい。（記載されている語の異なる形を用いるかもしれません）

例：Maurice / Ingrid / speak / loudly
Maurice speaks louder than Ingrid.「モーリスはイングリッドより大声で話す」

1. cats/dogs/run/fast

_____

2. my brother/your sister/write/beautiful

_____

3. you/I/learn/quick

_____

4. Rashad/Steven/sell/many cars

_____

5. New York/Chicago/big

_____

6. Ginger/Fred/dance/well

_____

7. lake/sky/look/blue

_____

8. our team/your team/play/capable

_____

9. the husband/the wife/seem/jealous

_____

10. Mr. Espinosa / Ms. VanDam / have/little money

_____

練習問題 20-3

イタリック体で書かれた語を最上級に変更してそれぞれの文を書き直しなさい。

1. Carlos is the *short* boy in the last row.

_____

2. Paris is *beautiful.*

_____

3. The white stallion runs *fast.*

_____

4. Is Russia a *large* country in Europe?

_____

5. Is this an *interesting* article?

_____

6. They say that the CEO is *rich.*

_____

7. Smoking is *bad* for your health.

_____

8. The soprano sings *softly.*

_____

9. The vice president spoke *brilliantly.*

_____

10. Is the planet Pluto *far?*

_____

11. Larry gets up *early.*

_____

12. She is *systematic* about everything she does.

_____

13. Brian is a *cute* boy.

_____

14. Laura plays the violin *well.*

_____

15. That book is *boring*.

練習問題20-4
語を文として書き直し、形容詞と副詞を最上級として形成し、必要な語を追加しなさい。

　例：Dennis / jump / high
　　Dennis jumps the highest.　　「デニスは一番高く跳ぶ」

1. Melanie/funny/girl/in class

2. what/distant/planet

3. your/handwriting/bad

4. men/at the party/eat/much

5. Olive/smart/all/girls/in school

6. Mozart/compose/beautiful/music

7. grandmother/bake/delicious/cake

8. pickpocket/steal/many/wallets

9. Raj/think/this symphony/boring

10. Janice/my/good/friend

練習問題20-5

それぞれの文を2度、最初の文は形容詞と副詞を比較級に、次の文は最上級に変更して書き直しなさい。

1. My coffee is hot.

_____

_____

2. Is this math problem difficult?

_____

_____

3. L feel well today.

_____

_____

4. Life in the jungle is dangerous.

_____

_____

5. This village is poor.

_____

_____

6. Mr. Hong always has little time.

_____

_____

7. The choir sang a merry song.

_____

_____

8. She wore a shabby dress.

_____

_____

9. Bert has many friends.

_____

_____

10. She can speak calmly about it.

_____

_____

Unit 21 | 接続詞

接続詞は、語、句、文を結び付けます。最初に、一般的に等位接続詞として用いられるいくつかの語を見てみましょう：例えば、*and, but, or, nor, for, so, yet*。注目、等位接続詞が、語、句、完全な文をどのように組み合わせるか：

組み合わせる語	組み合わせる句	組み合わせる文
"Don *or* Norma 「ドンまたはノルマ」	"healthy again *yet* unable to work" 「再び健康になったが、まだ働けない」	"We remained by the fire, *but* Lance went to the park to skate" 「私たちは火のそばに留まりましたが、しかし、ランスはスケートをするために公園に行きました」
"meat *and* potatoes" 「肉とジャガイモ」		

相関接続詞もまた重要です。相関接続詞は、同じ文の異なる部分に現れる単語のペアで構成されています。最も一般的に用いられるのは、both…and, either…or, neither…nor, not only…but also（時々、not only…alsoとして述べられる）です。例えば：

Both Yoko *and* Marco have problems. 「ヨウコとマルコは両方とも問題を抱えている」
Either you work hard *or* you leave. 「一生けん命働くか退職するか、どちらかにしなさい」
Neither the boys *nor* the girls wanted to end the game.
　　　　「少年たちも少女たちも、どちらも試合が終わって欲しくなかった」
You are *not only* a poor loser *but also* a bad soccer player.
　　　　「あなたは往生際が悪いばかりではなく、サッカー選手としてもお粗末だ」

従属節（あるいは従位接続詞）は主語と動詞から成り立っていますが、しかし、従属節は通常、単独では用いることはできません。従属節は、従位接続詞によって先導され、独立節と結び付きます。従位接続詞のリストは多いです。ここに最も一般的に用いられるいくつかを挙げます。

after	before	since	until
as if	how	than	when
as long as	if	that	whenever
as though	now that	though	where
because	once	unless	while

例文をいくつか見てください。

After she arrived, Alberto was the first to greet her.

「彼女が到着した後、アルベルトは彼女に最初に挨拶した」

Although he was tired, he continued to run.

「彼は疲れていたにもかかわらず、走り続けた」

I just don't know *how* you do it. 「どうやってやるか全くわからない」

If you don't pay your rent, you'll have to move.

「家賃を支払わない場合、引っ越ししなければならないでしょう」

Bob doesn't know *where* she lives. 「ボブは彼女の住んでいるところを知らない」

練習問題21-1

それぞれのペアの文を適切な等位接続詞を使って組み合わせなさい：and, but, or , nor, for, so, yet.

1. That's my brother. The woman next to him is his wife.

_____

2. We ran into the tent. Our clothes were already soaked by the storm.

_____

3. Should we watch TV tonight? Should we go see a movie?

_____

4. She began to cry. The book ended so sadly.

_____

5. I hurried as fast as I could. I arrived home late as usual.

_____

6. The red car was already sold. Kim bought the blue one.

_____

7. Our dog likes to play in the yard. Our cat prefers to stay in the house.

_____

8. Milo lives on Oak Street. His brother lives nearby.

_____

9. Their credit was very poor. They decided to buy a piano anyway.

_____

10. I love the snowy beauty of winter. I hate the heat of summer.

練習問題21-2

適切な相関接続詞を使って空欄を埋めなさい：both…and, either…or, neither…nor, not only…but also.

1. _____ Maribeth _____ I will ever visit them again.

2. I want to buy z _____ a new blouse _____ a new skirt.

3. They were already introduced to _____ Carol _____ her mother.

4. You _____ work too little _____ spend too much money.

5. _____ Father _____ Mother became ill during the cruise.

6. She wants _____ your help _____ your advice.

7. Reggie _____ broke his leh _____ bruised both arms.

8. It's always _____ too hot _____ too cold for you.

9. _____ the kitchen _____ the bathroom need to be cleaned.

10. _____ Cary _____ Kelly showed up at the party.

練習問題21-3

それぞれの従位接続詞を従える独立節を使ってそれぞれの文を完成させなさい。

1. She left for home after _____ .

2. When _____ , Pedro started to laugh.

3. I won't help you unless _____ .

4. Do you know where _____ ?

5. Once _____ , I was able to relax.

6. Chris closed the book before _____

7. You can stay up late as long as _____ .

8. While _____ , he relaxed under a tree.

9. I don't remember if _____

10. Now that _____ , they often go to the theater.

練習問題21-4
それぞれの下記の接続詞を使って２つの独自の文を書きなさい。

1. but _____

_____

2. unless _____

_____

3. neither…nor _____

_____

4. where _____

_____

5. how _____

_____

6. and _____

_____

7. not only…but also _____

_____

8. for _____

9. when _____

10. either…or _____

Unit 22 | 疑問詞

疑問詞とは疑問を問う語です。疑問詞は文頭に（あるいは近くに）置かれ、その文は語尾に疑問符が置かれます。疑問詞のいくつかは代名詞です：例えば、who, whom, whose, what, which。疑問詞は次の役割ができます：

　　・文の主語
　　・直接目的語
　　・前置詞の目的語
　　・所有格

それらの例を見てください：

主語：	Who is standing on the corner?	「誰が隅に立っていますか」
	Whose is for sale?（名詞主語は理解されている）	「誰のものが売りに出されていますか」
	What needs to be done?	「何をする必要がありますか」
	Which is for me?	「どちらが私のためですか」 あるいは「どちらが私のものですか」
直接目的語：	Whom did you see last night?	「昨夜、誰に会いましたか」
	Whose did you borrow?（名詞の目的語は理解されている）	「誰のものを借りましたか」
	What will they do?	「彼らは何をしようとしているのですか」
	Which have you selected?	「どちらを選びましたか」
前置詞：	With whom was she dancing?	「彼女は誰と踊っていたのですか」
	About whose was he speaking?（名詞は理解されている）	「彼は誰について話していたのですか」
	To what are you referring?	「何に言及しているのですか」
	In which is it located?	「それはどちらにありますか」
所有格：	Whose house burned down?（whose が house を修飾する）	「誰の家が全焼したのですか」

副詞の役割をする他の疑問詞：例えば、how, when, where, why.　いくつかの例：

疑問文	可能な解答
How did he walk?「彼はどのように歩きましたか」	slowly「ゆっくりと」

When was the party?「パーティーはいつでしたか」　　on Tuesday「火曜日に」

Where are you going?「どこへ行くところでしたか」　　to the store「店へ」

Why are you limping?「なぜ足を引きずって歩いてい　　because my foot hurts「足をけがした

るのですか」　　　　　　　　　　　　　　　　　からです」

また、what, which, howと他の語句とを組み合わせて一般的に用いられる句もいくつかあります。疑問文は他の疑問詞と同じようにそれらの語（what, which, how）で形成されます。

> what brand of（どのブランドの）, what kind of（どんな種類の）, what sort of（どんな種類の）, what about（どうですか）
>
> which one（どちらが）, which way（どちらの方法）, which part of（どの部分の）, which of you（あなた方のうち）,
>
> how much（いくら）, how many（いくつ）, how often（どのくらいの頻度で）, how about（どうですか）
>
> 〈※日本語の意味は代表的なもの〉

もちろん、このような組み合わせだけではありません。それらは例です。同じように形成されている他の例も見つかるでしょう。いくつかの例文：

What kind of dress do you want to buy?	「どんなドレスを買いたいですか」
What about your brother?	「弟さんはどうですか」
Which one is for me?	「どちらが私のためですか」
	あるいは「どちらのものが私のですか」
Which of you will help me?	「どちらが私を手伝ってくれますか」

疑問詞は、2つの節を結び付けるのに接続詞として用いることができます。接続詞についてはUnit21でそれらのいくつかと出会いました。しかし注意してください！　接続詞として疑問詞を用いることによって形成された文は、他の節と組み合わせた場合、必ずしも疑問文にはなりません。それは、疑問を問うているか供述しているか、どちらかによります。

疑問文	平叙文
Do you know who he is?	Jill told me who he is.
「彼が誰だか知っていますか」	「ジルは彼が誰かを教えてくれた」
Does she understand how it works?	I can't explain how it works
「それがどのように機能するか彼女は理解していますか」	「それがどのように機能するか説明できない」
Who told you where it was?	They couldn't discover where it was.

「それがどこにあったか誰が教えてくれました
たか」

Can you tell me what kind of car this is?

「これがどんな種類の車か教えてくれません
か」

「それがどこにあったか彼らは見つけること
ができなかった」

I don't know what kind of car this is.

「これがどんな種類の車か知りません」

注目：直接疑問文〈※一般疑問文〉と別の節と組み合わさった疑問詞節〈間接疑問文〉との間
の語順変化。直接疑問文では動詞が主語に先行するし、疑問詞節では動詞が主語の後に従いま
す。

Who *are* these people?

「これらの人々は誰ですか」

When *did* they *arrive*?

「彼らが到着したのはいつですか」

How far *can* he swim?

「彼はどれくらいの距離を泳げますか」

She asked me who these people *are*.

「彼女は私にこれらの人々は誰ですかとたずねた」

I don't know when they *arrived*.

「彼らがいつ到着したか知らない」

They ask how far he *can swim*.

「彼らは彼がどれくらいの距離を泳げるかとたず
ねている」

練習問題22-1

それぞれの文のイタリック体で書かれた語と語句を見なさい。それから、適切な疑問の語を
使って、その語に関連する疑問文を作りなさい。

例：*Thomas* is a friend of his.　　「トーマスは彼の友だちの一人です」

Who is a friend of his?　　「彼の友だちは誰ですか」

1. Lupita bought *a black* dress.

_____

2. Panama is located *in Central America*.

_____

3. She wanted to buy *a new hat and coat*.

_____

4. Kevin decided to go *home*.

_____

5. Kendall spent a lot of time talking *with his cousin*.

_____

6. She started to laugh *because the movie was so funny*.

_____

7. The man on crutches came down the steps *carefully*.

_____

8. The clock stopped *at precisely 10:42 A.M.*

_____

9. Ms. *Ewell* has worked for this company for years.

_____

10. My *sister's* husband is a firefighter.

_____

11. She should select *this* pair of gloves.

_____

12. There are *more than fifteen* people in the room.

_____

13. This dog is *a Chihuahua*.

_____

14. The *lion' presence* meant danger.

_____

15. Los Angeles is *either north or south* from here.

_____

練習問題 22-2
質問に最もよく答える太字体の語句を丸で囲みなさい。

1. Whose car is in the driveway? **your/the girl/Nikki's**

2. What's crawling on the wall? **there/a bug/their house**

3. When can you pick the children up? **tomorrow/here/at your house**

4. What brand of car did you buy? **a Ford/foreign/a new one**

5. Which one of them took the money? **him/that man/theirs**

6. How long is this plank? **several/more than/six feet**

7. Whom did he visit in Mexico? **the ocean/mountains/a friend**

8. Where is the village you come from? **for many people/near the sea/a little earlier**

9. How does your aunt feel today? **always/quickly/better**

10. Which part of the play didn't you understand? **the ending/of the actors/at the theater**

練習問題 22-3
適切な句を使ってそれぞれの文を完成させなさい。

1. I don't know why _____

2. With whom were you _____

3. He won't explain what kind of _____

4. Whose parents _____

5. What sort of man would _____

6. Andi told me what _____

7. It's hard to believe how _____

8. The accident happened when _____

9. How much _____

10. Which one of you _____

Unit 23 | 否定

noはyesの反対です。noは質問に対する否定の答えとして用いられます。しかし、英語にはまた、それ以外の否定の形もあります。

単純否定は、文中で活用変化された動詞の後にnotを置くことで生じます。単純否定が、notの位置を決定するのは活用変化された動詞であること、そして文中にまたあるかもしれない他の動詞的な形〈※準動詞の形など〉でないことを覚えるのは重要なことです。

He is *not* at home today.	「彼は、今日は家にいない」
We do *not* want to buy a car this time.	「私たちは今のところは、車を買いたいとは思わない」
Marianne has *not* responded to my letter.	「マリアンヌは私の手紙に返事をよこさない」

もし文が疑問文の形なら、notは主語の後ろに置かれる。

Can you *not* understand?	「分かりませんか」
How could he *not* have helped us?	「どうやっても彼は私たちを助けることはできなかったのですか」
Will Martin *not* share his good fortune?	「マーティンは幸運を分かち合わないのだろうか」

しかし、notを使った短縮形の場合には、短縮形の2つの部分は決して分離されません。
それは、文が平叙文であろうが疑問文であろうが関係ありません：

He *isn't* at home today.	*Can't* you understand?
「彼は今日家にいない」	「分かりませんか」
We *don't* want to buy a car.	Why *couldn't* he help us?
「車を買いたいとは思わない」	「なぜ我々を助けることができなかったのですか」
She *hasn't* answered yet.	*Won't* Martin share with us?
「彼女はまだ答えていない」	「マーティン、我々と分かち合えないのだろうか」

否定される動詞がbe, have, あるいは他の助動詞（can, should, must, など）でない場合は、否定形は動詞の時制に応じて、doの現在時制かまたは過去時制から形成されます。

I am not	I do not speak	「私は話せません」
she has not	she doesn't learn	「彼女は学べません」
you shouldn't	you did not understand	「あなたは分からなかった」

he can't he didn't worry 「彼は心配しなかった」

他の特定の否定語句には2つの形式があります。1つの形式はno-（neverとneitherを除く）で始まり、もう1つの形式はnotの後に別の語が続くことで構成されます。それらの語句が否定でない時、それらの語句は、語someをしばしば用いる特別な肯定の形になります。それが実在するさまざまな形を見てください。

no-を伴って構成される	notを伴って構成される	肯定の形
none	not any	some
no one	not anyone（あるいはanybody）	someone（あるいはsomebody）
nothing	not anything	something
nowhere	not anywhere	somewhere
never※	not ever	ever
neither※	not either	either

※つづりに注意する。

2つの形式の使用方法が異なることに注意してください。

I have *none* to give you. I do *not* have *anything* to give you.
「あなたに与えるものは何もありません」

He spoke to *no one*. He did *not* speak to *anyone*.
「彼は誰とも話さなかった」

We want *nothing* from you. We do *not* want *anything* from you.
「私たちはあなたから何も望みません」

She's *nowhere* to be found. She's *not anywhere* to be found.
「彼女はどこにも見当たらない」

I'll *never* forgive you. I will *not ever* forgive you.
「私はあなたを決して許しません」

He wants *neither* of them. He does not want *either* of them.
「彼はどちらも望んでいません」

否定語が文から削除されると、肯定的な形式がそれに取って代わります。

Hector didn't dance with anyone. → Hector danced with someone.
「ヘクターは誰もダンスをしてくれなかった」→「ヘクターは誰とでもダンスをした」
The customer wants nothing. → The customer wants something.
「お客は何も望んでいません」→「お客は何かを望んでいます」

注目：英語は、決して否定を重ねては用いない ― 例えば、doesn't want nothing.

練習問題23-1

最初はnotを追加し、次はnotの短縮形を用い、それぞれの文を2回書き直しなさい。

1. The boys were playing basketball at the park.

_____

_____

2. My sister is a concert pianist.

_____

_____

3. Are you well?

_____

_____

4. His nephew is learning Japanese.

_____

_____

5. Can they explain how this happened?

_____

_____

6. The judge ordered him sent to prison.

_____

_____

7. We will be traveling to Spain this summer.

_____

_____

8. Does Mr. Amin have our lawnmower?

_____

_____

9. My sister spends a lot of time in the library.

10. Judith understood the situation.

練習問題23-2

否定を削除して、それぞれの文を書き直しなさい。必要に応じて適切な肯定形式を用いなさい。

1. I haven't had enough time to work on this

2. 0000mark doesn't get to work on time.

3. She didn't bring her dog along.

4. Have you never been to New York City?

5. Lin wasn't speaking with anyone.

6. The children don't cooperate with the substitute teacher.

7. They don't live anywhere in the city.

8. Couldn't the horse run faster?

9. Marta didn't break the window.

10. No, I don't like this kind of music.

_____

11. Chase isn't dancing with anyone.

_____

12. Can't you find anything you need?

_____

13. I haven't written the proposal for them.

_____

14. No, she doesn't spend her vacation with us.

_____

15. He got nothing interesting in the mail.

_____

練習問題23-3
（　　　）内の否定語句を用いて創意に富んだ文を書きなさい。

1.（not）_____

2.（never）_____

3.（no one）_____

4.（not anywhere）_____

5.（not anything）_____

6.（none）_____

7.（not ever）_____

8.（neither）_____

9. (nowhere) _____

10. (nothing) _____

Unit 24 | 数詞

数詞は一般に量を具体的に述べるためと計算に用いられます。例えば、加算、減算、乗算、除算。これまでに多くの形でそれらと間違いなく遭遇しています。最初に基数を再検証してみましょう。

0	zero	21	twenty-one
1	one	22	twenty-two
2	two	30	thirty
3	three	40	forty
4	four	50	fifty
5	five	60	sixty
6	six	70	seventy
7	seven	80	eighty
8	eight	90	ninety
9	nine	100	one hundred
10	ten	101	one hundred one
11	eleven	102	one hundred two
12	twelve	200	two hundred
13	thirteen	500	five hundred
14	fourteen	1,000	one thousand
15	fifteen	2,000	two thousand
16	sixteen	10,000	ten thousand
17	seventeen	11,000	eleven thousand
18	eighteen	20,000	twenty thousand
19	nineteen	100,000	one hundred thousand
20	twenty	111,111	one hundred eleven thousand one hundred eleven

気を付けて！　かなり大きな数詞への英語の名称は、他の言語の名称とは異なります：

英語	数
million（100万）	1,000,000
billion（10億）	1,000,000,000
trillion（1兆）	1,000,000,000,000

数詞が方程式で用いられる時、用いられるべき一定の数学用語があります。加算では、数詞は語plus〈※　足す〉かand〈※　足す〉かのどちらかと組み合わされます。例えば、five plus

164

three （5 ＋ 3）, ten and nine （10 ＋ 9）。

減算では、方程式が語minus 〈※　～を引いた、－〉を用いることを要請します。例えば、ten minus four （10 － 4）。

乗算では、方程式が語times 〈※　掛ける、×〉を用いることを要請します。例えば、six times three （6 × 3）。

除算では、方程式は句divided by 〈※ 割り算する、÷あるいは/ 〉を要請します。twenty divided by five （20 ÷ 5 ）。

方程式がその中に等号（＝）を持っていたら、それはequals 〈※　イコール〉あるいはis （＝）として述べられています。例えば、two plus two equals four （2 ＋ 2 ＝ 4）, six minus three is three （6 － 3 ＝ 3）。

数詞が小数なら、小数は語point 〈※ 小数点〉で表現されます。例えば、6.5は "six point five （6.5）" のように言われます。また10.7は "ten point seven （10.7）" のように言われます。

序数詞はグループやシリーズ内の順位を示すものです。大部分の序数詞は、数の終わりに -th を加えることで形成されます。例えば、tenth, twentieth, sixty-seventh, hundredth, など。けれども、下記の5つの序数詞は記憶せねばならない特別なつづりを持っています。

1 ＝ first
2 ＝ second
3 ＝ third
5 ＝ fifth
12 ＝ twelfth

序数詞を伴う例文をいくつか挙げます：

We have three daughters, but Denise was our first.
「私たちには娘が3人いますが、デニスは最初の娘でした」
The second seating for dinner is at 8:30 P.M.
「2回目のディナーの着席は午後8時30分です」
She was born on the twenty-fifth of June.
「彼女は6月25日に生まれた」

日付は2つの方法で表現されます：May fifth または the fifth of May 〈※ どちらも5月5日〉。日

付を数詞で表す場合、日付の前に月を示すのが最も一般的です。例えば、9/11 = September eleventh（9月11日）、6/12 = June twelfth（6月12日）。他の多くの言語では、日付が月に先行します。このことが混乱を引き起こす原因となります。というのは、一部の人々は6/12を the sixth of December（12月6日）の意味にとります。英語を話す人にとって、その書き方は、一般的に June twelfth（6月12日）を意味します。このような混乱を避けるために、次の形式で日付を示すのが賢明です。例えば、June 12, 2005（2005年6月12日）。

序数は、また1/2以外の分数を表すためにも使用されます。

> 1/2 = one-half（2分の1）（序数ではない）
> 1/4 = one-fourth（4分の1）（注：one-fourth is sometimes expressed as "one-quarter" or "a quarter."「4分の1は、"one-quarter"（4分の1）あるいは "a quarter"（4分の1）として表現されることもあります」
> 1/3 = one-third（3分の1）
> 3/10 = three-tenths（10分の3）
> 14/25 = fourteen twenty-fifths（25分の14）（注意：付随する数が1より非常に大きい場合、序数の複数構成に注意）

2,000年より先に起こった年のことは、2つの部分で表現されます：1850年は、"eighteen fifty," のように、1066年は "ten sixty-six." のように呼ばれます。1999年以降の年は別の呼び方をします。

2000	two thousand
2001	two thousand one, or twenty oh one
2002	two thousand two, or twenty oh two
2010	two thousand ten, or twenty ten
2022	two thousand twenty-two, or twenty twenty-two

イベントが発生した日付を言う時、語onの使用は任意です。

> The boy was born *on* May first.　「その少年は6月1日に生まれた」
> The boy was born May first.

練習問題24-1
それぞれの方程式を言葉で書き直しなさい。

1. 5 + 7 = 12

2. 11 − 6 = 5

_____

3. 345 − 220 = 125

_____

4. 22 × 10 = 220

_____

5. 100 × 63 = 6,300

_____

6. 10,000/ 500 = 200

_____

7. 880 × 3 = 2,640

_____

8. 88,000 − 55,000 = 33,000

_____

9. 11.5 × 10 = 115

_____

10. 93.3/3 = 31.1

_____

練習問題 24-2

（　　）内の基数を適切な序数に変更しなさい。

1. Mr. Woo was born on the（2）_____ of October.

2. I'm sitting in the（4）_____ row.

3. My birthday was on the（21）_____ of July.

4. This is only the（3）_____ time we met.

5. The old woman died on her (100) _____ birthday.

6. They're celebrating their (30) _____ anniversary.

7. Who's the (5) _____ boy in line?

8. That was her 0810) _____ phone call today.

9. Mr. 000burton was their 081,00009 _____ customer and won prize.

10. Adam scored in the (99) _____ percentile.

11. I think 0i was (1) _____ in line.

12. 0our seats are in the (12) _____ row.

13. Christmas Day is always on the (25) _____ .

14. The old woman died on her (86) _____ birthday.

15. 0our new car arrived on the (22) _____ of August.

練習問題24-3

語として書かれた（　　）内に示された日付を使って、それぞれの文を完成させなさい。いずれの場合も、月が日付の前になります（例、5/2 = 5月2日）。

1. (8/10) She was born on _____

2. (10/12) He'll arrive on _____

3. (11/11) The party will be _____

4. (2/16/1999) He died on _____

5. (4/1/2002) They met on _____

6. (12/24) Christmas Eve is _____

7. (7/4) Where will you spend _____ ?

8. (1492) Columbus arrived in the New World in _____

9. (2/14/2004) The dance is _____

10. (6/2) Was the baby born on _____

Unit 25 いくつかの重要な対照

英語を勉強し、熟達すればするほど、良い文法規則を破ることを言うネイティブ・スピーカーがいることに気づくでしょう。英語について知れば知るほどますます、それが事実であることが分かります。すべての言語のネイティブは、さまざまなレベルの能力で話します。文法的にきわめて正確に話す人もいれば、よりカジュアルでただ不注意なだけで、良い言語の規則を無視する人もおります。

次の8組の単語について、ネイティブがどこで頻繁に間違いを犯すかを明らかにします。これらの語を知ることによって、英語をどのように話したらよいかを自分で選択できるようになります：つまり、正確に話したり書いたりするようになるし、あるいはカジュアルに、または無頓着な習慣に順応できるようになります。

Bad と Badly

badが形容詞であり、badlyが副詞であることは明らかです。しかし、英語のネイティブ・スピーカーの中には、badをもっぱら形容詞と副詞の両方で使う人がおります。この問題は、badが連結動詞（be, become, seem, appear, など）の後に続いた時、副詞のように見えるという事実におそらく起因しています。

That's too bad.	「それは残念です」
She looks bad this morning.	「彼女は今朝、具合が悪そうだ」

Unit 5 動詞の連結動詞で復習できます。

誰かが "That little boy reads and writes *bad*.「あの小さな男の子はひどい読み書きをする」" と言うのを聞くかもしれません。しかし、この用法では副詞が必要です。この文は "That little boy reads and writes *badly*「あの小さな男の子は読み書きがまずい」" とすべきです。badとbadlyを正しく用いるべき方法のいくつかの例を見てください：

You're a bad dog. （dogを修飾している形容詞）
　「いけない犬ね」
In bad weather we stay at home. （weatherを修飾している形容詞）
　「悪天候なので、家に留まっています」
Your cut isn't so bad. （連結動詞isの後ろに続く形容詞）
　「あなたのカットは割といい」
His reply sounded bad. （後に連結動詞soundedが続く形容詞）
　「彼の返事は不快に聞こえた」

You have a badly broken wrist.　　　　（分詞 broken を修飾している副詞）
　「手首をひどく骨折をされていますね」
They played badly today.　　　　（動詞 played を修飾している副詞）
　「彼らは今日、ひどいプレイをした」

Good と Well

この一組の単語は、bad や badly とほぼ同じ方法で、または、いくつかの同じ理由で誤用されています。しかし、good と well には余分な混乱を伴います。というのは、語 well は、その用い方によって、形容詞あるいは副詞のどちらかになり得るからです。well は good の副詞的な形であり、また good が形容詞として用いられた時は ill でないことを意味する語でもあります。

good は bad の反対であって形容詞です。注目、この語の形容詞と副詞の意味がどのように使用されているかに注意してください：

形容詞	副詞
Miguel is a *good* soccer player.	Miguel plays soccer *well*.
「ミゲルは優れたサッカー選手です」	「ミゲルはサッカーを上手にやっています」

もし good が " kind「親切な」," の意味であれば、その副詞的な部分として kindly「親切に」を用いることができます：

形容詞	副詞
David is a *good* man.	He always speaks so *kindly* of them.
「ダビデは善良な人です」	「彼はいつもそれらをとても親切に話します」

しかし、well が連結動詞と一緒に用いられた場合は、それは形容詞です。誰かが " I don't feel *good*."「気分が悪い」と言うのを聞くかもしれません。その用法は間違っています。というのは、ここでの意味は "not ill「病気ではない」" です。正しい使い方は "I don't feel well.「私は気分が悪い」" です。

しかし、good と well の話はこれで終わりではありません。これらの両方の語は連結動詞に従うことができ、その場合は、これらの両方の語は形容詞と見なされます。しかし、それらの意味は異なります：

連結動詞と一緒の文		意味すること	
She looks *good*.	「元気そうです」	She doesn't look bad.	「調子悪そうには見えない」
She looks *well*.	「体調良く見える」	She doesn't look ill.	「体調が悪いようには見えない」

They are *good.*　「彼らは優秀だ」　They aren't bad. OR They aren't unkind.
　　　　　　　　　　　　　　　　　　「悪くはない」あるいは、「不親切ではない」
They are *well.*　「彼らは元気です」　They aren't ill.　　「彼らは病気ではない」

Few と A few

この一対の語の違いは、そんなに大きくはありません。"Few men are strong enough.「十分に
強靭な強さの人はほとんどいない」"と言うのは正しい。"A few men are strong enough.「十分
に強靭な強さの人は、少しはいる」"ともまた言うことができます。しかし、この文の間に含
蓄するものにわずかな違いがあります。その違いを明瞭に示すいくつかの例を見せましょう。

文	含蓄
Few people saw this movie.	Not many people went to see this movie.
「この映画を見た人はほとんどいなかった」	「この映画を見に行った人はあまり多くない」
	(There is a negative implication here.)
	(「ここには否定の含蓄がある」)
A few people saw this movie.	Some people saw this movie but not a lot.
「何人かの人がこの映画を見た」	「この映画を見た人もいたが、しかし多くはな
かった」
	(The implication is more positive.)
	(「含蓄はより肯定的である」)
Few students understood him.	He was hard to understand.
「彼を理解した学生はほとんどいなかった」	「彼を理解するのは難しかった」
	(There is a negative implication here.)
	(「ここには否定の含蓄がある」)
A few students understood him.	Some of the students did understand him.
「学生の中には彼を理解したものもいた」	「学生の中には彼を本当に理解したものもいた」
	(This implication is more positive.)
	(「この含蓄はより肯定的である」)
She has few friends.	She has almost no friends.
「彼女には友だちがほとんどいない」	「彼女にはほとんど友だちがいない」
	(There is a negative implication here.)
	(「ここには否定の含蓄がある」)
She has a few friends.	She has some friends but not a lot.
「彼女には何人かの友だちがいる」	「彼女には何人かの友だちがいるが、しかし多
くはない」
	(This implication is more positive.)

（「この含蓄はより肯定的である」）

fewは物事について否定的な見方を暗示するのに用いなさい。a fewはより肯定的な見方を示すのに用いなさい。

Fewer と Less

多くの人々はこの2つの語を誤用します。しかし、それらの用法は極めて単純です：複数名詞を修飾するのにはfewerを用いなさい。単数名詞（そしてしばしば集合名詞）を修飾するのにはlessを用いなさい。fewerはfewの比較級でlessはlittleの比較級です。いくつかの例：

複数名詞	単数名詞
I have fewer books.	I have less money.
「本をほとんど持っていない」	「わずかなお金しか持っていない」
We need fewer jobs to do.	She has less time than usual.
「するべき仕事がわずかでも必要だ」	「普段より時間が少ない」
Fewer and fewer friends came to visit.	Mom has less and less patience with him.
「訪ねてくる友だちがますます少なくなった」	「お母さんは彼にだんだん我慢できなくなっている」

さて、これらの語の原級と比較級の形を比べてみましょう。

原級	比較級
He has few ideas.	He has fewer ideas than you.
「彼にはほとんどアイディアがない」	「彼はあなたよりアイディアが少ない」
February has few days.	February has fewer days than March.
「2月は日数が少ない」	「2月は3月より日数が少ない」
I have little time.	I have less time now than a year ago.
「ほとんど時間がない」	「今は1年前より時間が少ない」
She has little pain.	She has less pain today than yesterday.
「彼女は痛みがほとんどない」	「彼女は昨日より今日の方が、痛みが少ない」

Lay と Lie

この2つ語は多くの英語の話し手を混乱させます。layは他動詞で直接目的語をとります。lieは自動詞で直接目的語をとりませんが、しかし、しばしば場所を示す前置詞句が後に続きます。

He lays the baby on the bed.　　　　　　（他動詞 / 間接目的語 = baby）
　　「彼は赤ちゃんをベッドに寝かせる」
Where did you lay my book?　　　　　　（他動詞 / 直接目的語 = book）

「私の本をどこに置きましたか」

Hamburg lies on the Elbe River.　　　　　　（自動詞 / on を伴う前置詞句）

「ハンブルクはエルベ川沿いにある」

Your coat is lying over the railing.　　　　　（自動詞 / over を伴う前置詞句）

「あなたのコートは手すりにかけられています」

これら2つの動詞の間に混乱が生じるのは、この2つの動詞の活用のためです。すべての時制でそれらを比べてみて、lieの過去時制の特定のメモをとりなさい。

	lay	lie
現在形	he lays「〜を横たえる」	he lies「横たわる」
過去形	he laid「を横たえた」	he lay「横たわった」
現在完了形	he has laid「を横たえてしまった」	he has lain「横たわってしまった」
過去完了形	he had laid「を横たえてしまっていた」	he had lain「横たわってしまっていた」
未来形	he will lay「を横たえているだろう」	he will lie「横たわっているだろう」
未来完了形	he will have laid「を横たえてしまっているだろう」	he will have lain「横たわってしまっているだろう」

layとlieのどちらを使うべきかを決めるのが難しい場合、その動詞の代わりにputを使いなさい。意味が通じたら、layを使いなさい。意味が通じなかったら、lieを使いなさい。

He *puts* the baby on the bed.（意味が通じる）→ He *lays* the baby on the bed.

「彼は赤ちゃんをベッドに寝かせる」

She *puts* on the bed and sleeps.（意味が通じない）→ She *lies* on the bed and sleeps.

「彼女はベッドに横になって眠ります」

〈※　put onは、身につける、を着る、などの意味〉

Little と A little

この一対の語はfewとa fewに似ています。Littleには否定を含蓄する意味を持っています。a littleはより肯定的な見方を示します。いくつかの例です：

文	暗示
Little is known about him.	Not much is known about him.
「彼はほとんど知られていない」	「彼はあまり知られていない」
	(There is a negative implication here.)
	（「ここは否定を含蓄している」）
A little is known about him.	Something is known about him but not a lot.

「彼は、少しは知られている」	「彼はいくらか知られているがそれほどでもない」
	(This implication is more positive.)
	(「ここでの含蓄はより肯定的である」)
She does little work.	She doesn't work much.
「彼女はほとんど仕事をしない」	「彼女はあまり仕事をしない」
	(There is a negative implication here.)
	(「ここには否定の含蓄がある」)
She does a little work.	She does some work but not much.
「彼女はいくらか仕事をしている」	「彼女はいくらか仕事をしているが、たいしたことはない」
	(This implication is more positive.)
	(「ここでの含蓄はより肯定的である」)
He says little.	He doesn't say much.
「彼はほとんど話さない」	「彼はあまり話さない」
	(There is a negative implication here.)
	(「ここには否定の含蓄がある」)
He says a little.	He says something but not much.
「彼は、少しは話す」	「彼はいくらか話すが、たいしたことはない」
	(This implication is more positive.)
	(「ここでの含蓄はより肯定的である」)

Than と Then

早口の会話で、これらの語がほとんど同じように聞こえたとしても、取り違えることはほとんどありません。しかし、書く際には、これらの語は識別されなければなりません。than は前置詞や接続詞として用いることもできる上に、比較されている2つの要素の間に置くこともできます：例えば、Marisa is taller *than* Anthony. 「マリサはアンソニーより背が高い」、She runs faster *than* you do. 「彼女はあなたより速く走る」。

then という語は2つの大きな働きを持っております：(1) 副詞として用いて、when（時）の質問に答える。または (2) 接続詞として「結果として、またはその後は」の意味で2つの節を結び付けることもできます。これらの2つの働きを比較してみましょう。

副詞	接続詞
We were in Mexico then, too.	I found the book then returned to my room.
「我々も当時メキシコにいました」	「本を見つけてそれから部屋に戻した」
Then I decided to go to college.	She slapped his face, then she ran down the street.
「その時、大学へ行くことを決めた」	「彼女は彼の顔をひっぱたいて、それから通りを走り下りた」

Who と Whom

これら2つの語は頻繁に使われ、しばしば誤用されます。who は疑問文の主語として用いる形があります：

Who sent you? 「誰があなたを送ったの」
Who knows the man over there? 「あそこにいる男が誰だか知っていますか」

whom は直接目的語、間接目的語、あるいは前置詞の目的語として用いられます：

直接目的語 → Whom did you meet at the party? 「あなたはパーティーで誰に会いましたか」
間接目的語 → (To) Whom will you give an invitation? 「あなたは誰を招待するのでしょうか」
前置詞の目的語 → With whom was he siting? 「彼は誰と一緒に座っていましたか」

who と whom の再検討は Unit 22 の疑問詞の項を参照してください。

英語の多くのネイティブ・スピーカーが、whom を避けてもっぱら who を使うことを覚えておくことは重要なことです。

標準英語	カジュアルな英語
Whom did they arrest?	Who did they arrest?
「彼らは誰を逮捕したのですか」	「彼らは誰を逮捕したのですか」
From whom did you get the gift?	From who did you get the gift? または
「あなたは誰からその贈り物を貰いましたか」	Who did you get the gift from?
	「あなたは誰からその贈り物を貰いましたか」

正式に話したり書いたりする時には、who や whom の標準的な形を用いるべきです。カジュアルな手紙や会話では、裁判官になったつもりで whom を避けるべきです。

練習問題 25-1
2つの太字体の語のより良い方を丸で囲みなさい。

1. Today was a very **bad/badly** day at work.

2. The patient isn't doing **good/well** this morning.

3. He's an awful man. **Few/A few** people like him.

4. Tori has known **fewer/less** happiness in her later years.

5. Does your dog always **lay/lie** in that corner?

6. She's very ill, but we still have **little/a little** hope.

7. I believe this knife is sharper **than/then** that one.

8. **Who/ Whom** will you invite to dinner?

9. Her ankle is **bad/badly** swollen.

10. The condition of the well looks **good/well** again.

11. I'm not poor. I have **few/a few** dollars to give him.

12. You know **few/less** about her than I do.

13. If you **lay/lie** that on the shirt, you'll wrinkle it.

14. **Little/A little** kindness won't do him any harm.

15. I grabbed an umbrella **than/then** rushed out the door.

16. A long massage always feels **good/well**.

17. I know **fewer/less** men in this club than you.

18. Did you **lay/lie** my new skirt on the ironing board?

19. Why do you treat your pet so **bad/badly**?

20. You think you're smarter **than/then** I am.

練習問題 25-2
標準的な英語でそれぞれの文を書き直しなさい。

1. The little boy acted verb bad in class today.

2. Don't you feel good?

_____

3. Omar has friends than his brother.

_____

4. Mom is laying down for a while.

_____

5. Kris is prettier then Hilda.

_____

6. Who did you send the letter to?

_____

7. Were you in Europe than, too?

_____

8. I laid on the floor and played with the dog.

_____

9. Johnny plays good with the other children.

_____

10. Her voice sounds badly today.

_____

練習問題 25-3
（　　）内の語を用いて、標準的な英語で創意に富んだ文を書きなさい。

1. (bad) _____

2. (badly) _____

3. (good) _____

4. (well) _____

5. （few）_____

6. （a few）_____

7. （fewer）_____

8. （less）_____

9. （to lay）_____

10. （to lie）_____

11. （little）_____

12. （a little）_____

13. （than）_____

14. （then）_____

15. （who）_____

16. （whom）_____

復習用の練習問題3

本書のそれぞれの章の内容に対する力量をチェックするために、下記の練習問題を使用してください。練習の結果に満足できない場合は、適切な章を復習して、再度練習を行ってください。

練習問題R3-1
それぞれの文のイタリック体で書かれた語句を見なさい。それがどのように使用されているかを決めて、それから、空白に主語、直接目的語、間接目的語、前置詞の目的語、あるいは叙述主格のいずれかを書きなさい。

1. _____ I like dancing with *Maria.*

2. _____ Do you have *enough money* for the movies?

3. _____ Is *your sister* staying home tonight?

4. _____ My aunt sent *my mother* a beautiful bouquet.

5. _____ My older brother became *a teacher.*

6. _____ Uncle John is *a major* in the Air Force.

7. _____ *That e-mail* is from a friend in Spain.

8. _____ Tom wants to buy *a piano.*

9. _____ I lend *my cousin* twenty dollars.

10. _____ The young couple sits beside *the river.*

練習問題R3-2
定冠詞か不定冠詞か、どちらか適切な方で、空欄を埋めてください。

1. We greeted _____ tourists as they entered the room.

2. Where are _____ keys to this door?

3. Do you see _____ bus or a streetcar coming?

4. She has _____ difficult puzzle for you.

5. Do you want to order a pizza or _____ French fries?

6. What time does _____ plane land?

7. _____ teacher's name is Ms. Johnson.

8. Is that _____ rabbit hiding under the bush?

9. She really liked _____ story I wrote.

10. Can you read _____ sign over the entrance?

練習問題R3-3
文中で最も理にかなう太字体の形容詞を丸で囲みなさい。

1. Jack found a **long/several/wrong** board behind the garage.

2. The new school has a **large/young/quick** gymnasium.

3. The **former/boring/last** train leaves at 10:00 P.M.

4. That woman is very **long/old/final**.

5. We were watching a **careful/funny/gray** movie.

6. There was a **green/sad/empty** snake hiding in the shade.

7. That driver is just too **same/careless/red**.

8. I hope you can visit us at our **new/short/tall** apartment.

9. After the race, the athletes were **big/thirsty/simple**.

10. That **long/green/handsome** man is my cousin.

練習問題R3-4

提供された空欄に、太字体の語句にふさわしい代名詞を書きなさい。

1. I gave **Tom** a few extra dollars. _____

2. We found **these beautiful dishes** in France. _____

3. I hope you can send **my wife and me** a postcard. _____

4. My son never eats **broccoli**. _____

5. **Mr. Garcia** is the new manager of the store. _____

6. I'd like to introduce you to **Anna Keller**. _____

7. Are **the children** still asleep? _____

8. **A large rock** is in the middle of the driveway. _____

9. **The whole team** went out for pizza. _____

10. Do **Paul and I** have to do the dishes tonight? _____

練習問題R3-5

過去時制、現在完了時制、未来時制でそれぞれの文を書き直しなさい。

1 . I have a job in the city.

_____

_____

_____

2 . Do you like working for him?

_____

_____

_____

3. My mother wants to buy a new TV.

_____

4. He pins a medal on my chest.

5. Your husband needs to get more exercise.

6. Ashley does not drive.

7. The children are learning to write.

8. Are you well?

9. The man often breaks a dish.

10. Are your sons living together?

練習問題 R3-6

（　　）内の助動詞を使ってそれぞれの文を書き直しなさい。本来の文と同じ時制を保持しなさい。

1. I borrow some money from her.
   (to have to) _____
   (to need to) _____

2. We shall drive to New Orleans.
   (to be able to) _____
   (to have to) _____

3. You help your neighbors.
   (can) _____
   (ought to) _____

4. The boys were a little lazy.
   (can) _____
   (might) _____

5. The smallest children do not play here.
   (should) _____
   (must) _____

6. Do they work long hours?
   (to have to) _____
   (to want to) _____

7. I didn't perform in the play.
   (to want to) _____
   (could) _____

8. Jean leaves for Hawaii on Tuesday.
   (should) _____
   (may) _____

9. Will you stay with relatives?
   (to have to) _____

（to be able to）_____

10. Mr. Patel doesn't live in the suburbs.

（to want to）_____

（should）_____

練習問題R3-7

下記の能動態の文を受動態の文として書き直しなさい。同じ時制を保持しなさい。

1. Our broker will sell the house.

_____

2. Did your company build the new jetliner?

_____

3. My aunt is baking a cake.

_____

4. I located the island on this map.

_____

5. An earthquake destroys the village.

_____

6. Tom has written the e-mail incorrectly.

_____

7. Robert is carrying the baby into the nursery.

_____

8. No one saw the accident.

_____

9. Dr. Patel was examining the sick child.

_____

10. Won't a mechanic repair the car?

_____

（　　　）内の動詞を適切な仮定法の形として空欄を埋めなさい。

1. I demand that he _____ an I.D. right now.（to show）

2. She would be grateful if you _____ to help her.（to try）

3. If only my parents _____ here!（to be）

4. Thomas wishes he _____ enough money to take a vacation.（to have）

5. The lawyer suggested the woman _____ the document.（to sign）

6. If Mary _____ late, she wouldn't be able to meet the new student.（to arrive）

7. Ms. Nguyen would have learned English if she _____ here longer.（to live）

8. If only the man _____ been more careful.（to have）

9. If Tim had found the money he would _____ the bills.（to pay）

10. I recommended that you _____ allowed to live here a bit longer.（to be）

練習問題R3-9

文の（　　　）内の副詞を適切に配置しなさい。もし（　　　）内の語が形容詞であったら、それを副詞に変更し、その語を文中の適切な場所に置きなさい。

1. They never arrive.（punctual）

_____

2. Your brother is talented gymnast.（rather）

_____

3. A little puppy followed Jimmy.（home）

_____

4. The sergeant called the soldiers to attention.（harsh）

_____

5. Does your cousin sing?（good）

_____

6. The boys ran into the classroom.（fast）

_____

7. She was sleep and went home.（too）

_____

8. The man's voice was strong.（quite）

_____

9. Jane ran the race rapidly.（so）

_____

10. John stepped before the judge.（brave）

_____

練習問題R3-10
提供された空欄に、太字体の語句を短縮形として書きなさい。

1. We **must not** waste any more time. _____

2. **He would** really like this movie. _____

3. **I have** never seen such beautiful mountains. _____

4. **Did** you **not** get your homework done? _____

5. **They are** spending too much time at the mall. _____

6. **Who has** been using my laptop? _____

7. **I am** exhausted! _____

8. Tom **will not** be going to the dance. _____

9. **She will** find full-time work. _____

10. **It is** too cold today. _____

練習問題 R3-11

下記の文のそれぞれの名詞を複数形に変えなさい。動詞と冠詞に必要な変更を加えなさい。

1. Your best friend has always been your wife.

_____

2. The man has a painful broken tooth.

_____

3. A goose is paddling in the pond.

_____

4. That child is hiding in the box.

_____

5. The woman's foot was swollen.

_____

6. The person who caught the mouse is no hero.

_____

7. The deer was grazing in the field.

_____

8. Where is the leaf for the table?

_____

9. This lady wants to buy a fork and a knife.

_____

10. The ox roamed alongside the river.

_____

練習問題R3-12

それぞれの文の末尾に終止符、感嘆符、疑問符を置きなさい。

1. Did you have enough time to finish the project _____

2. Shut up now _____

3. My son turns ten years old tomorrow _____

4. Bob was asking whether I knew about the accident _____

5. Why did you break that lamp _____

それぞれの文を書き直し、必要と思われる個所にコンマを置きなさい。

6. Jane set books pens and documents on my desk.

_____

7. No it happened on June 28 2009.

_____

8. Grandfather dozed in a chair but grandmother worked in the kitchen.

_____

9. By the way you need flour butter and eggs for this recipe.

_____

10. My son was born on June 10 and my daughter on November 21 of the following year.

_____

練習問題R3-13

それぞれの文を見て、不定詞または動名詞がどのように用いられているかを決めて、提供された空欄に、名詞、動詞、副詞、形容詞のいずれかを書きなさい。

1. _____ My parents were *sitting* in the backyard.

2. _____ A swiftly *flowing* river can be dangerous.

3. _____ The car *to buy* should get good gas mileage.

4. _____ *Jogging* is great exercise.

5. _____ My youngest son doesn't like *swimming*.

6. _____ I bought her a necklace to *show* my love to her.

7. _____ We are *traveling* to Canada tomorrow.

8. _____ The *ending* of the movie was very sad.

9. _____ Bill was sent home from school for *cheating*.

10. _____ *To vote* is a citizen's obligation.

練習問題 R3-14
2番目の文を関係詞節に変更して、下記の一対の文を結び付けなさい。関係詞節としてthatを
使いなさい。

1. I haven't used the new pen. Tom bought me the new pen.

_____

2. They visited the city. Grandfather was born in the city.

_____

3. Have you met the athletes? I told you about the athletes.

_____

4. Maria showed me the math problem. She cannot understand the math problem.

_____

5. Bob has a good memory. His memory always serves him well.

_____

同じやり方に従って、関係代名詞としてwho, whom, whose, を用いなさい。

6. This is the man. The man's wife is a concert pianist.

_____

7. Let me introduce the guests. I told you about the guests yesterday.

_____

8. I was speaking with the young couple. The young couple's first child was born a week ago.

_____

9. She danced with the man. The man wrote a cookbook.

_____

10. Todd likes the girl. He met the girl at our party.

_____

練習問題 R3-15
それぞれの文の目的格の人称代名詞を主格の適切な再帰代名詞に取り換えなさい。

1. I was really proud of you.

_____

2. The squirrel sheltered them from the rain.

_____

3. She found him something good to eat.

_____

4. I don't like her in that dress.

_____

5. How did you injure him?

_____

6. The two boys forced us to finish the race.

_____

7. We are going to buy him some ice cream.

_____

8. Robert always pampered me.

_____

9. I had to ask him how that happened.

_____

10. The little girl always liked me in a pink dress.

_____

練習問題R3-16
イタリック体で書かれた所有格句を - 'sで終わる所有格に変えなさい。

例：The color *of the car* is red.
The car's color is red.

1. Do you have a picture of the father *of the bride*?

_____

2. This is the largest parking lot *of the city*.

_____

3. The office *of my doctor* is on the second floor.

_____

4. The value *of this factory* has gone up.

_____

5. The owner *of the puppies* could not be found.

_____

同じ指示に従うが、しかしイタリック体の句をofで作られた所有格に変えなさい。

例：The color *of the car* is red.
The *car's color* is red.

6. *The flower's* scent filled the living room.

---

7. *The nation's* wealth come from oil.

---

8. How do you explain *the children's* bad grades?

---

9. The judge could not understand *the document's meaning.*

---

10. Rabbits are often *the wolves'* prey.

練習問題 R3-17
それぞれの文をより分かりやすく完成させる太字体の語を丸で囲みなさい。

1. Did your girlfriend leave **my/her/hers** in her room?

2. The twins were visiting **ours/mine/their** relatives in Boston.

3. This bed is mine, and that one is **his/your/her**.

4. **Our/Yours/Mine** uncle was a ship captain.

5. No one in the classroom understood **one/her/theirs** lecture.

6. The injured pup licked **its/hers/theirs** paw.

7. Did you bring **your/mine/ours** sleeping bag?

8. I think you took **my/your/mine** by accident.

9. Jim found his passport, but where is **our/hers/their**?

10. Julie wants to borrow **hers/yours/my** car again.

練習問題 R3-18

それぞれの文をより分かりやすく完成させる太字体の語を丸で囲みなさい。

1. Two of the girls **was/is/are** new to our class.

2. Who is that sitting **next to/between/about** Ms. Garcia?

3. The **man/friend/men** I work with have been with the company for a year.

4. Several students **on/in/out** this class forgot about the test.

5. I have several gifts for **he/your/them**.

6. This letter **below/from/since** the major was a surprise.

7. I won't go to the party without **she/you/they**.

8. **Three/Several/One** of the actors wins an award.

9. An unfamiliar dog was running **off/toward/during** the child.

10. Only one **from/of/by** the boys will be chosen for the team.

練習問題 R3-19

大文字の使用を必要とするそれぞれの問題文の語句を書き直しなさい。

1. maria was born on July fifteenth in Chicago, Illinois.

_____

2. we like to spend every sunday with our grandparents in the city.

_____

3. will professor johnson give another speech on tax reform?

_____

4. during the winter jack often goes skiing in the mountains of Colorado.

_____

5. ms. Patel rarely drinks coffee or tea in the morning.

_____

6. when he visited the united states, he stayed at the Hilton hotel in new York.

_____

7. there was a terrible accident on main street on October first.

_____

8. the reporter wanted to speak to the president but was stopped by captain Wilson.

_____

9. everyone in the tenth grade liked reading _to kill a mocking bird_.

_____

10. governor shaw announced plans for new highways around the state.

_____

練習問題 R3-20
最初の文は形容詞および副詞を比較級に、次は最上級に変え、それぞれの文を２回書き直しなさい。

1. Our neighbors are rich.

_____

_____

2. They walked in the darkness carefully.

_____

_____

3. I have little patience with him.

_____

_____

4. Tina didn't feel well yesterday.

_____

_____

5. The tea was hot.

_____

_____

6. Tom ran slowly.

_____

_____

7. John and Ashley are my good friends.

_____

_____

8. The boys ate many cookies.

_____

_____

9. Was the play boring?

_____

_____

10. That man's language is bad.

_____

_____

練習問題 R3-21
それぞれの文を適切な節で完成させなさい。

1. The older dog likes to sleep a lot, but _____ .

2. When _____ , I often went to a Broadway show.

3. My neighbor said that _____ .

4. Jose and his wife live on the third floor, and _____ .

5. If you lose your driver's license, _____ .

6. _____ , so I stay out of the hot sun.

7. Did the woman ask you where _____ ?

8. Do you want to go shopping , or _____ ?

9. While I was living in Mexico, _____ .

10. He had no idea how _____

練習問題 R3-22

それぞれの文のイタリック体の語句を見て、次に、適切な疑問詞を使って、その語と関連する疑問文を作りなさい。

例：The car won't start again.　　「車は再び始動しないだろう」
　　What won't start again?　　「何で再始動しないでしょうか」

1. Guatemala is located in *Central America*.

_____

2. *Ms. Keller's* cat is hiding in the attic.

_____

3. I should try on *that* dress.

_____

4. He saw *more than twenty* injured people there.

_____

5. The next train arrives *in the early morning*.

_____

6. John's parents began to cry *because they were so proud of him*.

_____

7. *The woman standing on the corner* is waiting for a bus.

_____

8. You saw *several girls* playing soccer in the park.

_____

9. The angry look in his eyes meant *danger*.

_____

10. The hallway is *about ten feet long.*

_____

練習問題R3-23

最初の文はnotを追加することで、次に、notの短縮形を用いることで、それぞれの文を2回書き直しなさい。

1. The girls were chatting in the living room.

_____

_____

2. I am home before 7:00 P.M.

_____

_____

3. Are they coming to the dance?

_____

_____

4. Ashley spoke with Mr. Barrett about it.

_____

_____

5. Have the twins done tueir homework?

_____

_____

6. Does that woman see the car coming?

_____

_____

7. Tom will be spending the winter in Colorado.

_____

_____

8. Can you understand the lecture?

_____

_____

9. His fiancé sent his ring back.

_____

_____

10. Would you like to sit in the shade for a while?

_____

_____

練習問題 R3-24

語句として書かれた（　　）内に示された日付または数字をそれぞれの文で完成させなさい。月および日付の場合、月は日付に先行する（例えば、5/2―5月2日）。

1. Tomorrow is (6/30) _____ .

2. How much is (15 + 6) _____ ?

3. The man died on (11/5) _____

4. Who's the (3) _____ man in line there?

5. Her birthday was (10/2) _____ .

6. The party is on the (12) _____ of this month.

7. How much is (210 − 50) _____ ?

8. How much is (6.5 × 10) _____ ?

9. This is my (1) _____ driver's license.

10. Jack was their (500) _____ customer and won a prize.

練習問題 R3-25
それぞれの文をより分かりやすく完成させる太字体の語を丸で囲みなさい。

1. The blade on the long sword is sharper **than/then** on the short one.

2. It's a difficult text. **Few/Little/A few** people understand it.

3. John had a **bad/well/badly** time at school today.

4. You can **lay/laid/lie** the baby on the bed.

5. Only **much/a little/few** is known about the woman.

6. The patient had **laid/lie/lain** on his side for an hour.

7. That man talks a lot but says **less/little/fewer**.

8. A restful night's sleep is always **good/well**.

9. There are **few/less/fewer** people in the audience tonight than last night.

10. **Who/Whom** was supposed to meet Aunt Mary at the station?

付録：一般的な不規則動詞

現在時制	過去時制	過去分詞
am, are, is	was, were	been
become	became	become
begin	began	begun
bring	brought	brought
build	built	built
buy	bought	bought
choose	chose	chosen
cost	cost	cost
do	did	done
draw	drew	drawn
drink	drank	drunk
drive	drove	driven
eat	ate	eaten
fall	fell	fallen
feel	felt	felt
find	found	found
fly	flew	flown
forget	forgot	forgot,forgotten
get	got	got, gotten
give	gave	given
go	went	gone
grow	grew	grown
have, has	had	had
hear	heard	heard
hide	hid	hidden
hold	held	held
hurt	hurt	hurt
keep	kept	kept
know	knew	known
leave	left	left
let	let	let
light	lit, lighted	lit, lighted
lose	lost	lost

make	made	made
mean	meant	meant
pay	paid	paid
put	put	put
read	read	read
ride	rode	ridden
run	ran	run
say	said	said
see	saw	seen
sell	sold	sold
send	sent	sent
show	showed	shown
sing	sang	sung
sit	sat	sat
sleep	slept	slept
speak	spoke	spoken
stand	stood	stood
swim	swam	swum
take	took	taken
teach	taught	taught
tell	told	told
think	thought	thought
throw	threw	thrown
understand	understood	understood
wear	wore	worn
win	won	won
write	wrote	written

問題解答

Unit 1　名詞

1-1

1. 固有	6. 普通
2. 普通	7. 固有
3. 固有	8. 普通
4. 固有	9. 固有
5. 普通	10. 普通

1-2

1. glass	6. the store
2. Rocky Mountains	7. New York Times
3. Mexico	8. Roberto
4. Flowers	9. Professor Romano
5. bus	10. my books

1-3

1. 直接目的語	6. 間接目的語
2. 主語	7. 主語
3. 直接目的語	8. 述部名詞
4. 述部名詞	9. 直接目的語
5. 間接目的語	10. 直接目的語

1-4

模範解答

1. He likes my sister.	4. I gave the children some candy.
2. I want a new car.	5. I fed a puppy some meat.
3. Did you meet Jackie?	6. He sent Grandfather a gift.

1-5

1. The girl does not trust the boys.

2. Father often misplaces his wallet.

3. She always gives the landlord the rent money.

4. Anita wants to sell her new computer soon.

5. She buys her grandchildren the toys.

6. You must visit Ms. Johnson in New York.

7. They like their new house so much.

8. She can give little Johnny the present.

9. He needs to see Dr. Lee today.

10. She throws Michael the ball.

Unit 2 定冠詞と不定冠詞

2-1

1. a	6. the あるいは an
2. the	7. the
3. a	8. The あるいは A
4. the	9. the
5. −	10. a

2-2

1. They gave us oranges.

2. I like the books very much.

3. Do you often visit the farms there?

4. Rabbits are hiding behind it.

5. Katrina likes to play with the kittens.

6. Montel has a dog and a cat.

7. I want to buy the rose.

8. There is a gift for you.

9. Can you hear the baby crying?

10. Do you have a brother or a sister/

Unit 3 形容詞

3-1

1. late	6. handsome
2. little	7. early
3. young	8. terrible
4. fast	9. white
5. funny	10. Short

3-2

1. The song from Mexico was sad.

2. The story about a clown is funny.

3. The waiter out of work is careless.

4. The snake from Egypt is ugly.

5. The woman from Spain is beautiful.

3-3

模範解答

1. beautiful	6. old… thick
2. chocolate	7. New
3. interesting	8. Difficult
4. young	9. Little

5. good　　　　10. Strange

Unit 4　人称代名詞

4-1

1. you　　　　9. us
2. him　　　　10. them
3. She　　　　11. you
4. it　　　　12. I
5. me　　　　13. it
6. us　　　　14. us
7. We　　　　15. her
8. they

4-2

1. They　　　　6. her
2. it　　　　7. They
3. us　　　　8. it
4. they　　　　9. him
5. She　　　　10. it

4-3

模範解答

1. My friend and I　　　6. the teacher
2. the music　　　7. the girls
3. the books　　　8, the radio
4. My aunt　　　9. Elizabeth
5. Craig　　　10. the members

4-4

1. I sent it to my friends.　　　4. I didn't buy it for Ella.
2. She is giving them to us.　　　5. My brother will bring them to me.
3. They sold it to her.

4-5

1. me　　　　6. us
2. you　　　　7. them
3. him　　　　8. us
4. her　　　　9. us
5. it　　　　10. him

4-6

1. it　　　　5. him
2. them　　　　6. us

3. it   7. Them

4. her

Unit 5　動詞

1. 他動詞   6. 他動詞

2. 自動詞   7. 自動詞

3. 他動詞   8. 他動詞

4. 連結動詞   9. 連結動詞

5. 連結動詞   10. 他動詞

1. You rarely find a good book. / He rarely finds a good book.

2. She often makes mistakes. / they often make mistakes.

3. We go home early. / I go home early.

4. They can help us. / He can help us.

5. She does the dishes. / You do the dishes.

6. They must work tomorrow. / He must work tomorrow.

7. I borrow some money. / She borrows some money.

8. You send a few postcards. / We send a few postcards.

9. He can spend the night here. / They can spend the night here.

10. They grow very slowly. / He grows very slowly.

1. She has no money. / We have no money.

2. He is my cousin. / You are my cousin.

3. I am very sick. / She is very sick.

4. They have a new car. / He has a new car.

5. They are at home now. / She is at home now.

6. I am quite well. / He is quite well.

7. They have no tickets. / She has no tickets.

8. You have a new apartment. / He has a new apartment.

9. He is from Costa Rica. / I am from Costa Rica.

10. They have a big problem. / She has a big problem.

1. have   6. am

2. lives   7. Are

3. She   8. Has

4. are   9. Likes

5. It   10. She

5-5

1. Does Rocco's uncle live in Washington?

2. Is she his cousin?

3. Do we take this road to Chicago?

4. Are they in the garden?

5. Do I have your new address?

6. Am I your student?（Are you my student?）

7. Does Linda like Jack?

8. Do you buy flowers every day?

9. Does she sing beautifully?

10. Is it a nice day?

5-6

1. The boys are at home.

2. You want this book.

3. She has the money.

4. I am your friend now.

5. He goes there every day.

6. It is in there.

7. You understand English.

8. The boy feels better.

9. You are in the garden.

10. We have enough money.

5-7

1. Delores is not in the capital.

2. We do not have enough money now.

3. My father does not send him a postcard.

4. The books are not go there every day?

5. I do not go home late.

6. I am not an American.

7. The girls do not buy some ice cream.

8. We do not our homework.

9. Lisa does not like my cousin.

10. It does not seem very old.

5-8

1. Do you not have the time?

2. Does Mike not like this book?

3. Is Kent not at home?

4. Does he not go there every day?

5. Are the girls not happy?

6. Does Sean not speak Spanish?

7. Do the boys not make a cake for her/

8. Do they not do this very often?

9. Does mother not have enough money?

10. Am I not happy about it?

5-9

1. We always drive to New York.

2. She sometimes speaks quickly

3. I often work in the garden.

4. The boys frequently play tennis.

5. The women travel abroad every year.

6. Doug usually buys German beer.

7. Michelle always talks on the phone.

8. My brother sometimes sleeps in the living room.

9. They usually cook a roast.

10. His sister helps them every day.

5-10

1.She does understand the problem.

2. We do not go to the movies often.

4. Mac does not want to sell the old car.

5. Mr. Tyner does not write him a long letter.

3. I do like that dress.   6. The boys do work in this factory.

5-11

1. Susan helped her friends.   9. He caught the ball.

2. We went to the movies.   10. They played chess after supper.

3. She was washing the car.   11. Someone bad my wallet.

4. My father was in the kitchen.   12. Did Mr. Ibrahim live here?

5. She did not understand you.   13. They were learning a new language.

6. Were you satisfied?   14. Karen worked in New Orleans.

7. Did you always speak Spanish?   15. You often made mistakes.

8. The girls were riding on a horse.

5-12

1. He was writing a letter.   6. The boys were hurrying home.

2. My mother was sitting in the garden.   7. The dog was burying a bone in the yard.

3. Jim was standing next to Alicia.   8. I was having a bad day.

4. The man was bringing us some fish.   9. They were going to the store.

5. We were losing the game.   10. He was staying with an uncle.

5-13

1. Did they make some mistakes?

2. Did Will play a few games of cards?

3. Did the girls see the comet?

4. Did her aunt carry the basket into the kitchen?

5. Were they in the city all day?

6. Did Garth learn a good lesson?

7. Was she home all day?

8. Did Robert have the radio?

9. Did the woman run for the bus?

10. Did the dogs fight over a bone

5-14

1. Lana has been speaking with him.

2. Has he been going to his class?

3. I have been working all day.

4. The tourists have been flying around the world.

5. My parents have been walking along the river.

6. Has the boy been putting his toys away?

7. She has been teaching us all that she knows.

5-15

1. Ms. Nellum has taken the boy home.

2. We have ridden on a bus.

3. They have been riding their bikes.

4. Have you often made cookies?

5. She has not understood.

6. They have been doing their homework.

7. I have been going to the same class.

8. He often has broken his bat.

9. They have been breaking windows.

10. Juanita has written her a letter.

5-16

1. borrowed	6. Been
2. been	7. Been
3. Has	8. They
4. has	9. hurrying
5. listening	10. Written

5-17

1. Julio had written him a few letters.

2. I had been writing a novel.

3. Had you seen a doctor?

4. She had cut her finger.

5. The girls had stayed home again.

5-18

1. The woman had taken the girl home.

2. We had ridden on a train.

3. I had always spoken Spanish.

4. Had you often made roast beef?

5. Rebecca had not remembered.

6. Had he been doing his best?

7. I had been going to the movies.

8.Cindy had taught us English.

9. We had played the same game.

10. Bethany had written in her diary.

5-19

1. The girls will play soccer.

2. I will be learning to drive.

3. We will not be home on time.

4. Will you recognize him?

5. Trent will be driving to Texas.

6.The men will work many hours.

7. She will fly to London every year.

8.Dr. Saloff will not treat her asthma.

9. The little boy will lose his place.

10. Will he be going to the university.

5-20

1. My father will have taken the girl to school.

2. We will have ridden on the subway.

3. They will have been riding their bikes.

4. Will you have made candy?

5. She will not have understood.

6. Will they have done the work?

7. I will have been going to the same class.

8. Chet will have broken his finger.

9. She will have arrived by ten.

10. Sabrina will have written several notes.

5-21

1. Sig will have bought a car. / Sig has bought a car. / Sig had bought a car. / Sig will buy a car. / Sig will have bought a car.

2. I was helping them. / I have been helping them. / I had been helping them. / I will be helping them. / I will have been helping them.

3. We came home late. / We have come home late. / We had come home late. / We will come home late. / We will have come late.

5-22

1. Bill is going to take a class at the university. / Bill used to take a class at the university.

2. We are going to travel to Germany. / We used to travel to Germany.

3. I am going to have lots of parties. / I used to have lots of parties.

4. Are you going to live in Ecuador? / Did you used to live in Ecuador?

5. The children are going to watch television every evening. / the children used to watch television every evening.

6. Is she going to spend a lot of money? / Did she used to spend a lot of money?

7. They were going to sell the old SUV.

8. Liz was going to begin her studies at the university.

9. The twins were going to live together in San Francisco.

10. Was the attorney going to find a new witness?

Unit 6 助動詞

6-1

1. Serena can buy a new car. / Serena wants to buy a new car.

2. We can borrow some money. / We want to borrow some money.

3. I can leave at ten o'clock. / I want to leave at ten o'clock.

4. The boys can have cereal for breakfast. / The boys want to have cereal for breakfast.

5. My sister can be home by 6:00 P.M. / My sister wants to be home by 6:00 P.M.

6. They can travel to California. / They want to travel to California.

7. Mr. Gutierrez can carry the groceries for her. / Mr. Gutierrez wants to carry the groceries for her.

6-2

1. You stay in bad all day.

2. I try hard.

3. My brother is a little late.

4. We find a room for the night.

6. Ramon remains at home today.

7. They learn to behave well.

8. Do you hear me?

9. His girlfriend sells her condo.

5. Ms. Brown gets out of bed today.   10. Do you work every day?

6-3

1. Mr. Weston has to drive to Arizona.

2. We needed to borrow some tools from him.

3. I wanted to leave for Mexico on the tenth of May.

4. Ms. McAdam will be able to help you.

5. Jolene ought to repair the car.

6. Could you understand them? / あるいは Were you able to understand them?

7. Aaron was supposed to work on Saturday.

8. She must order the cake today.

9. Have you been able to fill out the application?

10. Our neighbors will want to paint their house.

Unit 7　受動態

7-1

1. Glenda is being kissed by Stuart.

2. She was being spoiled by her parents.

3. My eyes are being tested in the clinic.

4. They were being arrested for a crime.

5. Monique is being awarded a medal.

6. The treasure was being buried on an island.

7. The dog is being punished again.

8. Was the old barn being burned down?

7-2

1. We have been punished by Father.

2. The men have been taken prisoner.

3. She has been thanked by the happy tourists.

4. I have been beaten by a robber.

5. The car has not been washed again.

6. Tony has been examined by the doctor.

7. They have been surrounded by the enemy.

8. Has your sister been fired from her job?

9. Has the baby been carried to his bedroom?

10. She has been congratulated by her boss.

7-3

1. The cottage was destroyed by a storm.

2. Was the New World discovered by Columbus?

3. Our house will be bought by them.

4. The cakes have been baked by my grandmother.

5. The bread is being cut by Phil.

6. The newspapers were being sold by Sergio.

7. Has the money been taken by Iris?

8. The baby will be kissed by her.

9. Is the fence being built by Max?

10. The map was forgotten by her brother.

Unit 8   仮定法

8-1

1. She demands Forrest return home by 5:00 P.M.

2. The man suggests you wear a shirt and tie to work.

3. They requested I be a little more helpful.

4. My father demanded we pay for the damage to the car.

5. Did he suggest she come in for an interview?

6. Roger demands that the boy have enough to eat.

7. Did Mother request that her will be read aloud?

8. He has suggested that we be trained for other jobs.

9. Who demanded that the statue be erected on this site?

10. Did he suggest the mayor find a new assistant?

8-2

模範解答

1. … she be on time.   4. … he behave himself.

2. … you stay here tonight.   5. … he forget about this?

3. … I help him out.

8-3

1. I wish Becca were here today.

2. I wish we were having a big party for Grandmother.

3. I wish he had enough money to buy a condo.

4. I wish my friends had come for a visit.

5. I wish Darnell didn't need an operation.

6. I wish his uncle drove slowly.

7. I wish I could borrow some money from you.

8. I wish the weather were not so rainy.

9. I wish they helped me every day.

10. I wish she wanted to go on vacation with me.

8-4

1. … Garrett would ask her out.   6. … it were Erin's birthday.

2. … I would go to the store.

3. … he would near you.

4. … I would turn on the heat.

5. … he would help me wash the car.

7. … he liked the neighborhood.

8. … someone had a soccer ball.

9. … I lived in Puerto Rico.

10. … the baby were sick.

8-5

1. She would have sold me her bicycle if she had bought a new one.

2. If you had come early, you would have met my cousin.

3. If only Karen had been here.

4. The children would have played in the yard if it had not been raining.

5. If the lawyer had found the document, he would have won this case.

6. If only my mother had been able to walk again.

7. Juanita would have traveled to New York if she had gotten the job.

8. If he had found the wallet, he would have given it to Rick.

9. Jackie would have wanted to come along if he had had more time.

10. If only they had understood the problem.

Unit 9 副詞

9-1

1. walked timidly

2. quietly sat down

3. rather angrily

4. entered the classroom
   あるいは noisily entered

5. too boring

6. talked harshly

7. followed the pretty girl home

8. very smart

9. plays the piano well

10. coldly stared

9-2

模範解答

1. He very neatly stacked the books on the shelf.

2. You sing well.

3. She spoke sadly about the tragedy.

4. You're too weak.

5. He said it rather quickly.

6. I was there yesterday.

7. She never lied to me.

8. The man expressed his beliefs quite strongly.

9. You wrote that too carelessly.

10. She played the song to beautifully.

復習用の練習問題1

1. 間接目的語

2. 主語

3. 前置詞の目的語

4. 直接目的語

5. 直接目的語

R1-2

模範解答

1. Are these people from Mexico City?

2. The embarrassed boy sent her a long letter.

3. These are the puppies that were born last week.

4. The salesman found us the perfect, little house.

5. Ms. Olson spoke with your parents about the problem.

R1-3

1. the

2. the

3. a

4. the

5. （indefinite plural）

R1-4

1. The girls like playing with the puppy.

2. Does John have sons?

3. I want to buy a lamb chop.

4. Raccoons are hiding under our porch.

5. My neighbors gave me the keys to their house.

R1-5

1. blue

2. sad

3. beautiful

4. spacious

5. handsome

6. terrible

7. tall

R1-6

1. long

2. fur

3. difficult

4. sad

5. new

6. tiny

7. best

8. expensive

R1-7

1. you

2. her

3. me

4. it

5. them

6. I

7. us

R1-8

1. they are very friendly.

2. She is from Puerto Rico.

3. Have you met them yet?

4. May I use it for a few house?

5. Laura is anxious to meet him.

6. Juan sent us a book from Portugal.

7. It was lying at the bottom of the drawer.

8. Do they work in this office?

R1-9

1. 自動詞

2. 連結動詞

3. 連結動詞

4. 他動詞

5. 他動詞

R1-10

1. went / gone

2. liked / liked

3. was, were / been

4. gave / give

5. threw / thrown

R1-11

1. 進行中で

2. 習慣的な

3. 強調的な

4. 習慣的な

5. 進行中で

R1-12

1. We must wash the car every Saturday.

2. The children are singing sweetly.

3. The patient is able to get out of bed for a while.

4. Bill had broken the mirror accidentally.

5. The boys are supposed to prepare supper tonight.

6. Have you been able to fill out the application?

7. Jean wanted to paint her mother's portrait.

8. Are you being funny?

9. We will need to visit them at Christmas.

10. My aunt will have to drive to Los Angeles.

R1-13

1. His grandmother is kissed by Mark.

2. The old church was painted white by three men.

3. Three people have been arrested.

4. A cottage on the lake will be bought by me.

5. A delicious soup is being made by my uncle.

R1-14

1. Several men were forced into the back of the truck.

2. Magazines have been sold here every day.

3. The little girl will be spoiled by grandfather.

4. Had the women been interrogated?

5. His prize mare was awarded the grand prize.

R1-15

1. would end

2. had been

3. return

4. be

5. came

6. be

7. were

8. would help

9. If

10. would

R1-16

1. where

2. where

3. modifier

4. when

5. how

6. 修飾語

7. 修飾語

8. how

R1-17

模範解答

1. very

2. well

3. extremely

4. finally

5. rather

6. up the stairs

7. tomorrow

Unit 10　短縮形

10-1

1. You've	9. We've
2. I'm	10. I'll
3. He'd	11. She's
4. They're	12. Who'd
5. It's	13. You're
6. She'll	14. They've
7. Who's	15. It's
8. He's	

10-2

1. mustn't	6. Didn't
2. can't	7. wasn't
3. won't	8. don't
4. couldn't	9. Isn't
5. aren't	10. shouldn't

10-3

模範解答

1. He hasn't left for work yet.	6. I've been here a long time.
2. You mustn't do that.	7. He'll help us.
3. I shouldn't help you.	8. They're very good friends.

4. You needn't be so rude.　　　9. You'd like my brother.

5. Weren't you at the game yesterday?　　10. She's quite ill again.

Unit 11　複数形

11-1

1. houses
2. wives
3. oxen
4. foxes
5. teeth
6. mice
7. fezzes
8. persons / people
9. candies
10. vetoes
11. deer
12. factories
13. leaves
14. universities
15. juries

11-2

1. The boys are chasing the little mice.

2. His brothers are putting the pots in the boxes.

3. Do the teachers know the men?

4. The heroes of the stories were children.

5. My friends was to buy the knives, spoons, and dishes.

6. Geese are flying over the fields.

7. The clumsy persons / people hurt my feet.

8. The poor women have broken teeth.

9. We saw wild oxen in the zoos.

10. The ugly witches wanted the trained wolves.

Unit 12　句読法

12-1

1. She took a book from the shelf and began to read.

2. Do you like living in California?

3. She asked me if I know her brother.

4. Sit down and make yourself comfortable.

5. Shut up!

6. How many years were you in the army?

7. I can't believe it's storming again!

8. When did they arrive?

9. Watch out!

10. Her little brother is about eight years old.

12-2

1. Ms. Muti, please have a seat inmy office.

2. She bought children, ham, bread, and butter.

3. By the way, your mother called about an hour ago.

4. Paul was born on May 2, 1989, and Caroline was born on June 5, 1989.

5. No, you may not go to the movies with Rich!

6. Well, that was an interesting discussion.

7. The men sat on one side, and the women sat on the other.

8. Oh, the dress, hat, and gloves look beautiful on you, Jane.

9. It happened on April 5, 1999.

10. Yes, I have a suitcase and flight bag with me.

12-3

1. There are some things you need for this recipe: sugar, salt, and flour.

2. She understood the meaning of the story: Thou shalt not kill.

3. Peter is an excellent swimmer; he coaches a team at our pool.

4. This document is important; it will prove his innocence.

5. Add these names to the list: Irena Helen, Jaime, and Grace.

12-4

1. She asked, "Why do you spend so much money?"

2. I learned that from "Tips for Dining Out" in a restaurant magazine.

3. Rafael said, "Elena's grandfather is very ill."

4. "This is going to be a big problem," he said sadly.

5. Kurt will say, "The Ransom of Red Chief in school."

12-5

1. The geese's eggs are well hidden.

2. She can't understand you.

3. Is Mr. Hancock's daughter still in college?

4. The two girls' performance was very bad.

5. Ms. Yonan's aunt still lives in Mexico.

6. She met several M.D.'s at the party.

7. Do you know Mr. Richards?

8. The women's purses were all stolen.

9. He won't join the other Ph.D.'s in their discussion.

10. It isn't right to take another man's possessions.

12-6

1. Blake, will you please try to understand my problem?

2. They went to England, Wales, and Scotland.

3. Someone stole my money!

4. She asked, "When is the train supposed to arrive?"

5. Mr. Wilson's son wants to buy a house in Wisconsin.

6. I have the following documents: a will, a passport, and a visa.

7. Grandmother died September 11, 1999.

8. Jack is a pilot; he flies around the world.

9. Well, I can't believe you came home on time.

10 Are you planning another vacation?

Unit 13　不定詞と動名詞

13-1

1. 副詞　　　　4. 副詞

2. 名詞　　　　5. 名詞

3. 形容詞

13-2

1. 形容詞　　　6. 名詞

2. 動詞　　　　7. 形容詞

3. 形容詞　　　8. 動詞

4. 名詞　　　　9. 名詞

5. 名詞　　　　10. 名詞

Unit 14　関係代名詞

14-1

1. I found the money that belonged to Jack.

2. She has a good memory that always serves her well.

3. This is the woman that I told you about.

4. I have a document that proves my innocence.

5. They want to visit the country that Marsha comes from.

6. This is the doctor who saved my life.

7. Do you know the musician whom I met in Hawaii?

8. She like the gentleman whom I was telling her about. または She likes the gentleman about whom I was telling her.

9. I visited the sisters whose father had recently died.

10. Jerod noticed the stranger at whom all the neighbors were staring. または Jerod noticed the stranger whom all the neighbors were string at.

11. Pablo threw away the picture which the boys had found.

12. I have in the house in which my grandfather was born.

13. He bought a suit which is navy blue.

14. Anna has a new hat which I like very much.

15. He wanted to paint the bench on which a man was sitting. または He wanted to paint the bench which a man was sitting on.

14-2

模範解答

1. ⋯about whom they wrote so much.

2. ⋯that is located in Asia.

3. ⋯ whom you invited.

4. ⋯ in which I placed the eggs?

5. ⋯ that was so funny.

6. ⋯ whom you told me about.

7. ⋯ whose book was published.

8. ⋯ whom my uncle had worked for.

9. ⋯ blouse that has dark purple buttons.

10. ⋯ whose passports were lost.

14-3

1. He was in the city I visited last year.

2. Did you finally meet the woman I was telling you about?

3. Ron sold the house he was born in.

4. My father lost the checkbook he kept his credit card in.

5. Did you find the ball I threw over the fence?

6. That's the pretty girl I wrote this poem for.

7. I don't know the people he gave the flowers to.

8. The hat the magician pulled a white rabbit from was empty.

9. She forgot the tickets she had placed next to her briefcase.

10. They live in a tiny village we finally located on a map.

Unit 15　再帰代名詞

15-1

1. You found yourself in a difficult situation. / He found himself in a difficult situation. / She found herself in a difficult situation. / We found ourselves in a difficult situation. / They found themselves in a difficult situation. / Amy found herself in a difficult situation.

2. I enjoyed myself at the party. / You enjoyed yourselves at the party. / He enjoyed himself at the party. / She enjoyed herself at the party. / They enjoyed themselves at the party. / The boys enjoyed themselves at the party.

3. I am going to be very proud of myself. / My friends are going to be very proud of themselves. / Mother is going to be very proud of herself. / they are going to be very proud of themselves. / We are going to be very proud of ourselves. / Abdul and Ricky are going to be very proud of themselves.

4. You just couldn't help yourselves. / He just couldn't help himself. / She just couldn't help herself. / We just couldn't help ourselves. / They just couldn't help themselves. / The men just couldn't help themselves.

15-2

1. Jerry liked himself in the new suit.

2. They busied themselves with several different tasks.

3. We were very proud of ourselves.

4. She is buying herself a few new outfits.

5. The children hurt themselves.

6. I have to ask myself what to do now.

7. The young woman told herself not to give in.

8. He wants to find himself something nice to wear.

9. You've harmed no one but yourself（yourselves）.

10. The lizard hid itself under a rock.

Unit 16　所有格

16-1

1. the storm's center

2. the victims' condition

3. my classmates' behavior

4. the lab's equipment

5. each man's efforts

6. the animals' many illnesses

7. the young lawyer's documents

8. the roses' scent

9. the little bear cub's mother

10. the town's northern border

Unit 17　所有代名詞

17-1

1. The car on the corner is mine.

2. Was this yours?

3. The invading soldier searched theirs.

4. Did Dee find here?

5. Ours have lived in Brazil for a long time.

6. His is fair with everyone.

7. These problems are entirely his.

8. I need yours.

9. Mine is going to raise the rent.

10. Theirs made no sense.

17-2

1. The women want to visit their relatives in Europe.

2. She takes her children for a long walk.

3. Do you have tools in the truck?

4. I sent my address and telephone number to the office.

5. We want ours.

6. The picture fell out of its frame.

7. They spend their time in Canada.

8. Are you selling yours?

9. I left some papers in my apartment.

10. Jose found his wallet under the bed.

17-3

1. your	6. her
2. his	7. ours
3. his	8. His
4. theirs	9. its
5. mine	10. my

Unit 18　前置詞

18-1

1. The man next to him is a senator.

2. Did they leave after it?

3. Evan was dancing with her.

4. Why did you leave the house without it?

5. Are there washers and dryers in them?

6. Juan had some nice wine for them.

7. The man with her is her new boyfriend.

8. A large bear was coming toward him.

9. The letter from them made me very happy.

10. In spite of all them, Tonya went on smiling.

18-2

1. is	6. has
2. women	7. makes
3. needs	8. need
4. was	9. don't
5. need	10. captures

Unit 19　大文字使用

19-1

1. John, Cadillac

2. Is, Colonel Brubaker, Governor Dassoff

3. The, March, Buffalo

4. We, Chicago

5. In, Whittier School, St. James Park

6. She, February, E.F. Hutton, New York

7. Ms. Assad, Texas

223

8. Are, Mr., Mrs. Germak, Britney

9. Ted, Coke

10. The, The Adventures, Huckleberry Finn, May

11. His May, Cleveland Memorial Hospital

12. Mia, A.M.

13. Do

14. If, Mayor Yamamoto

15. We, New York Times, Sunday

19-2

1. May tenth, eighteen sixty-five

2. November eleventh, nineteen eighteen

3. July fourth, seventeen seventy-six

4. December twenty-fourth, two thousand

5. January first, nineteen ninety-nine

6. Nine A.M.

7. Eleven thirty P.M.

8. Six forty-five A.M.

9. seven fifty P.M.

10. eight fifteen A.M.

復習用の練習問題2

R2-1

1. he isn't

2. we'd

3. they've

4. I shouldn't

5. who's

6. it's

7. we're

8. he doesn't

9. I'm

10. she'll

R2-2

1. The factories are old.

2. He chased the little mice.

3. His foot is big.

4. Where are your brothers?

5. The wives sit on the sofa.

6. The leaf is falling already.

7. I met the woman in Toronto.

8. Did he use vetoes?

9. I found the sharp knife.

10. Did they find the old oxen?

R2-3

1. comma, period

2. exclamation point, exclamation point

3. question mark

4. quotation mark, comma

5. apostrophe, period

6. semicolon, period

7. colon, comma

8. quotation mark, question mark

9. comma, period

10. period

R2-4

1. to make

2. to read

3. living

4. getting

5. boring

6. to show

7. hiking, to hike

8. ending

9. to visit

10. chirping

R2-5

1. This is the jacket that belonged to Maria.

2. What is the country that Max came from?

3. Did you meet the woman that I met in Madrid?

4. I found the money that he hid in the attic.

5. He learned another language, which is a difficult task.

6. Where's the box, in which I put the books?

7. I spoke with the boy, whose sister is a police officer.

8. This is the gentleman I gave my passport to.

9. Is that the hat he carried the message in?

10. That's the girl I really like.

R2-6

1. I really enjoyed myself.

2. She really enjoyed herself.

3. They really enjoyed themselves.

4. You were happy with yourselves.

225

5. We were happy ourselves.

6. Who was happy with himself?

7. The twins were happy with tjemselves.

8. I couldn't help myself.

9. Tina couldn't help herself.

10. John and Mike couldn't help themselves.

R2-7

1. The woman's health was good.

2. The storm's end was a relief.

3. The bees' buzzing scares her.

4. Are the German Shephard's pups healthy?

5. I don't like that child's behavior.

R2-8

1. The shouting of the boys disturbed him.

2. Are those elks the prep of the lion?

3. The western border of the town is Main Street.

4. The condition of the victim grew worse.

5. Where are the instruments of the doctor?

R2-9

1. Is the car down the street yours?

2. Tom wanted mine.

3. She danced with everyone.

4. Its nest was behind a rock.

5. Jane found ours in the basement.

R2-10

1. John took his dog for a walk.

2. The photograph slipped out of its frame.

3. His students made Mr. Connelly proud.

4. I rarely spend my time sleeping.

5. Will you visit your friends in Washington?

Unit 20　比較級と最上級の形

20-1

1. This freight train is moving slower. または This freight train is moving more slowly.

2. My younger brother is mathematician.

3. Where is the older man you told me about?

4. Fanny swims better, but she still cannot dive.

5. Hunter's cold is worse today.

6. They have more to do before the end of the day.

7. I think have Robbie is more intelligent.

8. The new employee is more careless about his work.

9. She has more friends in the city.

10. This project is more critical to the success of the company.

11. Clarice just can't speak quieter. または Clarice just can't speak more quietly.

12. We have a bigger house out in the country.

13. Do you think that kind of language is more sinful?

14. The inn is farther down this road.

15. Your friend is more reckless.

20-2

1. Cats run faster than dogs.

2. My brother writes more beautifully than your sister.

3. You learn quicker than I do.

4. Rashad sells more cars than Steven.

5. New York is bigger than Chicago.

6. Ginger dances better than fred.

7. The lake looks bluer than the sky.

8. Our team plays more capably than your team.

9. The husband seems more jealous than the wife.

10. Mr. Espinosa has less money than Ms. VanDam.

20-3

1. Carlos is the shortest boy in the last row.

2. Paris is the most beautiful.

3. The white stallion runs the faster.

4. Is Russia the largest country in Europe?

5. Is this the most interesting article?

6. They say that the CEO is the richest.

7. Smoking is the worst for your health.

8. The soprano sings the softest.

9. The vice president spoke the most brilliantly.

10. Is the planet Pluto the farthest?

11. Larry gets up the earliest.

12. She is the most systematic about everything she does.

13. Brian is the cutest boy.

14. Laura plays the violin the best.

15. That book is the most boring.

20-4

1. Melanie is the funniest girl in class.

2. What is the most distant planet?

3. Your handwriting is the worst.

4. The men at the party ate the most.

5. Olive is the smartest of all the girls in school.

6. Mozart composed the most beautiful music.

7. Grandmother baked the most delicious cakes.

8. This pickpocket stole the most wallets.

9. Raj thinks this symphony is the most boring.

10. Janice is my best friend.

20-5

1. My coffee is hotter. / My coffee is the hottest.

2. Is this math problem more difficult? / Is this math problem the most difficult?

3. I feel better today. / I feel the best today.

4. Life in the jungle is more dangerous. / Life in the jungle is the most dangerous.

5. This village is poorer. / This village is the poorest.

6. Mr. Hong always has less time. / Mr. Hong always has the least time.

7. The choir sang a merrier song. / The choir sang the merriest song.

8. She wore a shabbier dress. / She wore the shabbiest dress.

9. Bert has more friends. / Bert has the most friends.

10. She can speak more calmly about it. / She can speak the most calmly about it

Unit 21　接続詞

21-1

1. That's my brother, and the woman next to him is his wife.

2. We ran into the tent, but our clothes were already soaked by the storm.

3. Should we watch TV tonight, or should we go see a movie?

4. She began to cry, for the book ended so sadly.

5. I hurried as fast as I could, but（または yet）I arrived home late as usual.

6. The red car was already sold, so Kim bought the blur one.

7. Our dog likes to play in the yard, but our cat prefers to stay in the house.

8. Milo lives on Oak Street, and his brother lives nearby.

9. Their credit was very poor, but（または yet）they decided to buy a piano anyway.

10. I love the snowy beauty of winter, but I hate the heat of summer.

21-2

1. Neither… nor	6. both… and / neither… nor
2. either…or	7. not only… but also

3. both… and

8. either… or

4. not only… but also

9. Neither… nor / Not only… but also

5. Neither… nor / Both… and

10. Neither… nor / Both… and

21-3

模範解答

1. She left for home after she graduated from college.

2. When she told another joke, Pedro started to laugh.

3. I won't help you unless you make some effort.

4. Do you know where Stephan put his wallet?

5. Once the kids were in bed, I was able to relax.

6. Chris closed the book before he got to the end.

7. You can stay up late as long as you get up on time tomorrow.

8. While I weeded the garden, he relaxed under a tree.

9. I don't remember if I turned off the coffee pot.

10. Now that they live in the city, they often go to the theater.

21-4

模範解答

1. I like the beach, but the water is cold. She's smart, but she's vain.

2. I'll quit unless you pay me more. We're going home unless the weather gets better.

3. Neither the husband nor the wife understood me. I want neither your time nor your money.

4. Do you know where she lives? I found out where you hid the money.

5. I don't know how you konew that. Tell me how I can fix ythe car.

6. He is my friend and helps me with everything. Alex is a mechanic, and Minnie is a teacher.

7. She's not only bright but also talented. I not only fell down but also tore my shirt.

8. I fought in the battle, for it was the right thing to do. The children were tired, for they had been busy all day.

9. He has no idea when the movie starts. This dog always knows when it's dinner time.

10. Either you find a job, or you find a new place to live. The songs were either too loud or too soft.

Unit 22　疑問詞

22-1

1. What kind of dress did Lupita buy/

2. Where is Panama located?

3. What did she want to buy?

4. Where did Kevin decide to go?

5. With whom did Kendall spend a lot of time talking?

6. Why did she start to laugh?

7. How did the man on crutches come down the steps/

8. When did the clock stop?

9. Who has worked for this company for years?

10. Whose husband is a firefighter/

11. Which pair of gloves should she select?

12. How many people are in the room/

13. What breed is this dog?

14. What mean danger/

15. Where is Los Angeles from here?

22-2

1. Nikki's	6. six feet
2. a bug	7. a friend
3. tomorrow	8 near the sea
4. a Ford	9. better
5. that man	10. the ending

22-3

模範解答

1. ···. you said that.

2. ···. speaking at the meeting?

3. ··· problems he has.

4. ··· brought the food to the picnic?

5. ···. do such a thing?

6. ··· you were planning to do.

7. ···they managed to escape.

8. ··· a car pulled in front of me.

9. ··· did you have to pay for it?

10. ···is going to help us?

Unit 23　否定

23-1

1. The boys were not playing basketball at the park. / The boys weren't playing basketball at the park.

2. My sister is not a concert pianist. / My sister isn't a concert pianist.

3. Are you not well? / Aren't you well/

4. His nephew is not learning Japanese. / His nephew isn't learning Japanese.

5. Can they not explain how this happened? / Can't they explain how this happened?

6. The judge did not order him sent to prison. / The judge didn't order him sent to prison.

7. We will not be traveling to Spain this summer. / We won't be traveling to Spain this summer.

8. Does Mr. Amin not have our lawnmower? / Doesn't Mr. Amine have our lawnmower?

9. My sister does not spend a lot of time in the library. / My sister doesn't spend a lot of time in the library.

10. Judith did not understand the situation. / Judith didn't understand the situation.

23-2

1. I have had enough time to work on this.

2. Mark gets to work on time.

3. She brought her dog along.

4. Have you ever been to New York City?

5. Lin was speaking with someone.

6. The children cooperate with the substitute teacher.

7. They live somewhere in the city.

8. Could the horse run faster?

9. Marta broke the window.

10. Yes, I like this kind of music.

11. Chase is dancing with someone.

12. Can you find something you need?

13. I have written the proposal for them.

14. Yes, she spends her vacation with us.

15. He got something interesting in the mail.

23-3

模範解答

1. I do not understand.

2. They never help me.

3. No one saw the accident.

4. It's not anywhere to be found.

5. He does not have anything for you.

6. None of your work correct.

7. He has not ever been in Europe.

8. She bought neither purse.

9. The thief was nowhere to be seen.

10. Uma knows nothing about math.

Unit 24 　数詞

24-1

1. Five plus seven is twelve.

2. Eleven minus six is five.

3. Three hundred forty-five minus two hundred twenty equals one hundred twenty-five.

4. Twenty-two times ten equals two hundred twenty.

5. One hundred times sixty-three is six thousand three hundred.

6. Ten thousand divided by five hundred is two hundred.

7. Eight hundred and eighty times three equals two thousand six hundred and forty.

8. Eighty-eight thousand minus fifty-five thousand is thirty-three thousand.

9. Eleven point five times ten is one hundred fifteen.

10. Ninety-three point three divided by three equals thirty-one pointone.

1. second
2. fourth
3. twenty-first
4. third
5. one hundredth
6. thirtieth
7. fifth
8. tenth
9. one thousandth
10. ninety-ninth
11. first
12. twelfth
13. twenty-fifth
14. eighty-sixth
15. Twenty-second

24-3

1. August tenth
2. October twelfth
3. November eleventh
4. February sixteenth, nineteen ninety-nine
5. April first, two thousand two
6. December twenty-fourth
7. July fourth
8. fourteen ninety-two
9. February fourteenth, two thousand four
10. June second

Unit 25　いくつかの重要な対照

25-1

1. bad
2. well
3. Few
4. less
5. lie
6. a little
7. than
8. Whom
9. badly
10. good
11. a few
12. less
13. lay
14. A little
15. then
16. good
17. fewer
18. lay
19. badly
20. than

25-2

1. The little boy acted very badly in class today.
2. Don't you feel well?
3. Omar gas fewer friends than his brother.
4. Mom is lying down for a while.

232

5. Kris is prettier than Hilda.

6. To whom did you send the letter/

7. Were you in Europe then, too/

8. I lay on the floor and played with the dog.

9. Johnny plays well with the other children.

10. Her voice sounds bad today.

25-3

模範解答

1. this is a bad situation.

2. They played badly today.

3. She's a very good mother.

4. I don't feel well.

5. I have few reasons to doubt you.

6. We have a few things to discuss.

7. There are fewer boys than girls.

8. She has less time now.

9. I'll lay it on the table.

10. He was lying on the floor.

11. There is so little money left.

12. I have a little time to spare.

13. You're younger than Barry.

14. I got up then took a shower.

15. Who is that stranger?

16. Whom will the boss promote/

復習用の練習問題3

R3-1

1. 前置詞の目的語

2. 直接目的語

3. 主語

4. 間接目的語

5. 叙述主格

6. 叙述主格

7. 主語

8. 直接目的語

9. 間接目的語

10. 前置詞の目的語

R3-2

1. the	6. the
2. the	7. The
3. a	8. a
4. a	9. the
5. —	10. The

R3-3

1. long	6. green
2. large	7. careless
3. last	8. new
4. old	9. thirsty
5. funny	10. handsome

R3-4

| 1. him | 6. her |

2. them   7. they

3. us   8. It

4. it   9. They

5. He   10. we

R3-5

1. I had a job in the city.

   I have had a job in the city.

   I will have a job in the city.

2. Did you like working for him?

   Have you liked working for him?

   Will you like working for him?

3. My mother wanted to buy a new TV.

   My mother has wanted to buy a new TV.

   My mother will want to buy a new TV.

4. He pinned a medal on my chest.

   He has pinned a medal on my chest.

   He will pin a medal on my chest.

5. Your husband needed to get more exercise.

   Your husband has needed to get more exercise.

   Your husband will need to get more exercise.

6. Ashly did not drive.

   Ashley has not driven.

   Ashley will not drive.

7. The children were learning to write.

   The children have been learning to write.

   The children will learn to write.

8. Were you been well?

   Have you been well?

   Will you be well?

9. The man often broke a dish.

   The man has often broken a dish.

   The man will often break a dish.

10. Were your sons living together?

    Have your sons been living together?

    Will your sons be living together?

R3-6

1. I have to borrow some money from her.

   I need to borrow some money from her.

2. We shall be able to drive to New Orleans.

   We shall have to drive to New Orleans.

3. You can help your neighbors.

   You ought to help your neighbors.

4. The boys can be a little lazy.

   The boys might be a little lazy.

5. The smallest children should not play here.

   The smallest children must not play here.

6. Do they have to work long hours/

   Do they want to work long hours?

7. I didn't want to perform in the play.

   I couldn't perform in the play.

8. Jean should leave for Hawaii on Tuesday.

   Jean may leave for Hawaii on Tuesday.

9. Will you have to stay with relatives?

   Will you be able to stay with relatives?

10. Mr. Patel doesn't want to live in the suburbs.

   Mr. Patel shouldn't live in the suburbs.

R3-7

1. The house will be sold by our broker.

2. Was the new jetline built by your company?

3. A cake is being baked by my aunt.

4. The island was located by me on this map.

5. The village is destroyed by an earthquake.

6. The e-mail has been written incorrectly by Tom.

7. The baby is being carried into the nursery by Robert.

8. The accident was seen by no one. / The accident wasn't seen by a anyone.

9. the sick child was being examined by Dr. Patel.

10. Won't the car be repaired by a mechanic?

R3-8

1. show	6. arrived, would arrive
2. tried	7. had lived
3. were	8. had
4. had	9. have paid
5. sign	10. be

R3-9

1. They never arrive punctually.

2. your brother is a rather talented gymnast.

3. A little puppy followed jimmy home.

4. The sergeant harshly called the soldiers to attention. / The sergeant called the soldiers to attention harshly.

5. Does your cousin sing well?

6. The boys ran into the classroom fast.

7. She was too sleepy and went home. / She was sleepy and went home too.

8. The nan's voice was quite strong.

9. Jane ran the race so rapidly.

10. John bravely stepped before the judge. / John stepped before the judge bravely.

R3-10

1. mustn't	6. Who's
2. He'd	7. I'm
3. I've	8. won't
4. Didn't	9. She'll
5. They're	10. It's

R3-11

1. Your best friends have always been your wives.

2. The men have painful broken teeth.

3. Geese are paddling in the ponds.

4. those children are hiding in the boxes.

5. The women's feet were swollen.

6. The people who caught the mice are no heroes.

7. The deer were grazing in the fields.

8. Where are the leaves for the tables?

9. These ladies want to buy forks and knives.

10. The oxen roamed alongside the rivers.

R3-12

1. Did you have enough time to finish the project?

2. Shut up now!

3. My son turns ten years old tomorrow.

4. Bob was asking whether I knew about the accident.

5. Why did you break that lamp?

6. Jane set the books, pens, and documents on mt\y desk.

7. No, it happened on June 28, 2009.

8. Grandfather dozed in a chair, but grandmother worked in the kitchen.

9. By the way, you need flour, butter, and eggs for this recipe.

10. My son was born on June 10 and my daughter on November 21 of the following year.

R3-13

1. 動詞
2. 形容詞
3. 形容詞
4. 名詞
5. 名詞
6. 副詞
7. 動詞
8. 名詞
9. 名詞
10. 名詞

R3-14

1. I haven't used the new pen that Tom bought me.

2. They visited the city that Grandfather was born in.

3. Have you met the athletes that I told you about?

4. Maria showed me the math problem that she cannot understand.

5. Bob has a good memory that always serves him well.

6. This is the man whose wife is a concert pianist.

7. Let me introduce the guests, about whom I told you yesterday. / Let me introduce the guests, whom I told you about yesterday.

8. I was speaking with the young couple, whose first child was born a week ago.

9. She danced with the man who wrote a cookbook.

10. Told likes the girl, whom he met at our party.

R3-15

1. I was really proud of myself.

2. The squirrel sheltered itself from the rain.

3. She found herself something good to eat.

4. I don't like myself in that dress.

5. How did you injure yourself?

6. The two boys forced themselves to finish the race.

7. We are going to buy ourselves some ice cream.

8. Robert always pampered himself.

9. I had to ask myself how that happened.

10. The little girl always liked herself in a pink dress.

R3-16

1. Do you have a picture of the bride's father?

2. This is the city's largest parking lot.

3. My doctor's office is on the second floor.

4. this factory's value has gone up.

5. The puppies' owner could not be found.

6. The scent of the flowers filled the living room.

7. The wealth of the nation comes from oil.

8. How do you explain the bad grades of the children?

9. The judge could not understand the meaning of the document.

10. Rabbits are often the prey of the wolves.

R3-17

1. hers	6. its
2. their	7. your
3. his	8. mine
4. Our	9. hers
5. her	10. my

R3-18

1. are	6. from
2. next to	7. you
3. men	8. One
4. in	9. toward
5. them	10. of

R3-19

1. Maria / July / Chicago / Illinois	6. When / United States / Hilton Hotel / New York
2. We / Sunday	7. There / Main Street / October
3. Will Professor Johnson	8. The / Captain Wilson
4. During / Jack / Colorado	9. Everyone / To kill / Mocking Bird
5. Ms. Patel	10. Governor Shaw

R3-20

1. Our neighbors are rich / richer / the richest.

2. They walked in the darkness carefully / more carefully / most carefully.

3. I have little / less / the least patience with him.

4. Tima didn't feel well / better / the best yesterday.

5. The tea was hot / hotter / the hottest.

6. Tom ran slowly / more slowly / the most slowly.

7. John and Ashley are my good / better / best friends.

8. The boys ate many / more / the most cookies.

9. Was the play boring / more boring / the most boring?

10. That man's language is bad / worse / the worst.

R3-21

模範解答

1. The older dog likes to sleep a lot, but the puppies spend their time playing.

2. When I visited New York City, I often went to a Broadway show.

3. My neighbor said that there was a terrible fire on Main Street.

4. Jose and his wife live on the third floor, and his parents live on the fourth floor.

5. If you lose your driver's license, you should apply for a new one immediately.

6. I often get sunburned, so I stay out of the hot sun.

7. Did the woman ask you where you found her purse?

8. Do you want to go shopping, or do you want to stay home and watch TV?

9. While I was living in Mexico, I took a few classes to learn Spanish.

10. He had no idea how I did the magic trick.

R3-22

1. Where is Guatemala located?

2. Whose cat hiding in the attic?

3. Which dress should I try on?

4. How many injured people did he see there?

5. When does the next train arrive?

6. Why did John's parents begin to cry?

7. Who is waiting for a bus?

8. Whom did you see playing soccer in the park?

9. What did the angry look in his eyes mean?

10. How long is the hallway?

R3-23

1. The girls were not chatting in the living room.

   The girls weren't chatting in the living room.

2. I am not home before 7:00 P.M.

   I'm not home before 7:00 P.M.

3. Are they not coming to the dance?

   Aren't they coming to the dance/

4. Ashley did not speak with Mr. Barrett about it.

   Ashley didn't speak with Mr. Barrett about it.

5. Have the twins not done their homework?

   Haven't the twins done their homework?

6. Does that woman not see the car coming?

   Doesn't that woman see the car coming?

7. Tom will not be spending the winter in Colorado.

   Tom won't be spending the winter in Colorado.

8. Can you not understand the lecture?

   Can you understand the lecture?

9. His fiancée did not send his ring back.

   His fiancée didn't send his ring back.

10. Would you not like to sit in the shade for a while?

    Wouldn't you like to sit in the shade for a while/

1. Tomorrow is June thirtieth.

2. How much is fifteen plus six?

3. The man died on November fifth.

4. Who's the third man in line there?

5. Her birthday was October second.

6. The party is on the twelfth of this month.

7. How much is two-hundred and ten minus fifty?

8. How much is six point five times ten/

9. This is my first driver's license.

10. Jack was their five-hundredth customer and won a prize.

1. than	6. lain
2. Few / A few	7. little
3. bad	8. good
4. lay	9. fewer
5. a little	10. Who

この本を翻訳するに当たり、下記の参考書からいろいろ参考にさせてもらいました。
ここに謹んで御礼申し上げます。

記

『ロイヤル英文法 改訂新版（旺文社)』

『新マスター英文法書（聖文新社)』

『INSPIRE 総合英語（文英堂)』

『総合英語 Forest 7th EDITION（桐原書店)』

『改訂版 英文法総覧（開拓社)』

Ed Swickは、英語の問題を解決し、より優れた英語を書きます：習うより慣れよ、英語の代名詞と前置詞：習うより慣れよ、を含めて、ESlプログラムの多数の経験豊富な著者です。

訳者プロフィール

伊藤 淳一（いとう じゅんいち）

岩手県出身、花巻市在住。
専修大学卒業後、バベル翻訳専門職大学院（USA）修了。
毎日、英文法の翻訳に生きがいを感じて生活しています。

著書
『英文ライティングのための実践英文法〔翻訳書〕』（バベルプレス 2014 年 9 月 15 日）

英語学習者のための英文法
PRACTICE MAKES PERFECT　English Grammar for ESL Learners

2021年 6 月30日　初版第 1 刷発行

著　者　Ed Swick
訳　者　伊藤 淳一
発行者　瓜谷 綱延
発行所　株式会社文芸社
　　　　〒160-0022　東京都新宿区新宿1－10－1
　　　　　　　　　　電話 03-5369-3060（代表）
　　　　　　　　　　　　 03-5369-2299（販売）

印刷所　図書印刷株式会社

ISBN978-4-286-21211-1